THE BLOSSOMS ARE GHOSTS AT THE WEDDING

THE BLOSSOMS ARE GHOSTS AT THE WEDDING

Expanded Edition

Tom Jay

Empty Bowl
Anacortes, Washington

New & Expanded Edition

First American printing in 2006.

Empty Bowl, founded in 1976 as a cooperative letterpress publisher, has produced periodicals, broadsides, literary anthologies, collections of poetry, and books of Chinese translations. As of 2018, our mission is to publish the collected works of poets who share Empty Bowl's founding purpose, "literature and responsibility," and its fundamental theme, the love and preservation of human communities in wild places.

Library of Congress Control Number 2019948504
ISBN 978-0-912887-83-8

Empty Bowl
Anacortes, Washington
www.emptybowl.org

Printed at Gray Dog Press
Spokane, Washington

Book design: Tonya Namura

All photographs by Mary Randlett.
(University of Washington Libraries, Special Collections, Mary Randlett, photographer, Mary Randlett Photograph Collection)

Table of Contents

Introduction

How do you describe Tom Jay? I wonder. Accomplished sculptural artist, foundry man, essayist, etymologist, environmentalist/restorer of salmon habitat, woodcutter, home builder, social and art critic, poet, philosopher/naturalist, water-witcher/well digger, counselor/friend; he's all of these things. A reading of the collection of his work in *Blossoms Are Ghosts at the Wedding* will likely have you conclude he's much more.

In the early 1970s, I met Tom Jay at a small cabin he was renting off a dirt road in the second-growth timber above Chimacum, Washington. I had sought him out as the *go to guy* for guidance as I prepared to model and then cast my first bronze. A narrow path led to his door and he was taking a lunch break from the construction of his own cabin and foundry across the road. First impressions tend to remain, and I recall the way his frame filled the doorway when he got up to greet me. He was at once formidable and inviting, dressed in workman's overalls complete with suspenders, and his bright eyes and a great smile were framed amid a corona of bushy hair and a full beard. He certainly looked to be a woodsman—one of the designations Jay has further defined throughout his life.

In the years ahead I would come to know this man well through the many personal and professional endeavors we worked on together. We dug footings in basalt for a studio foundation, took a cross-country camping trip to an art museum opening, floated rivers amid salmon runs, and plunged the depths for abalone along the edges of the Straits of Juan de Fuca. We counseled one another on some of the inevitable challenges that involve family, business and health. Enduring friendships are the fruit that sweetens and enriches a life. Such has been the case with Tom Jay. Our lives evolved together and independently. My first bronze work, Raven Into Flight, was modeled, cast, finished and installed by his soon-to-become River Dog Foundry. Though it was four decades ago, there is an indelible memory of the twelve hours we spent, through a long night, tending the wood fires required to burn out our plaster molds that held the waxes of the raven piece. Our long conversations that night were accompanied by the constant calls of screech owls and tree frogs that bantered back in forth from the deep woods around us.

Like Thoreau, Tom has sought to do his living *deliberately*. Close to nature, he has apportioned his time, energy and skills in a manner that ensures compatibility with his chosen place while staying open to all the lessons that can accrue from the experience. In poem, essay and opinion Tom transcribes what he has thought and learned. These musings are held together by a constant thread of reference to salmon, their diversity, and their irreplaceable role in human life and the life around them. In his essay "Homecoming," the tiny "eyed" forms within a pair of chum salmon eggs cradled in an egg box seem to watch him as he peers down upon them in "the smooth rhythmic shade of the water flow." He concludes that they are "the eyes of the watershed, venerable and rejuvenant in the same moment." Elsewhere, sharing company with a dying chum salmon when river swimming, he sees the fish as "crossing over to the other side, watershed specter, feeding the firs, subterranean sometime king, tree born elder, tutor." Here is a chronicle of a man coming together with his finned brethren in a common watershed to forge and employ a model for recovery. A restoration of a landscape haunted by salmon, "sea bright silver shuttles weaving our rain green world." His vision of the salmon is realized in his castings of bells that depict these cycles of life and in his monumental salmon forms found near sea- and riverside settlements of Western Washington. Incorporating Northwest cultural myths, his extraordinary bronze, "*Salmon Woman*" in Bellevue, Washington, brings forward the fullness of his heartfelt philosophy.

While the salmon of biology, myth and culture are prominent points of emphasis, it's also intriguing to explore the writer's poems of passion and reflections on commitments that have historically tied us to one another and the realities of the earth's resources. In a section of poems, discover the depth of love for his family and in particular his life's partner, Sara Mall. As a reader I was reminded of how important the combined strength of two people is to fulfilling the possibilities of living. Consider too the details of *water witching*, where one's inherent potential and then basic skill combine to provide a means of finding this element so fundamental to our existence. Join Jay in hand digging a water well and feel the determined and laborious process. Through his senses, put your hands into the earth and discover the distinctions between dirt and soil. To do all this the author remains at his woodlands home. Here he has exchanged "wheels for roots," to join in the creation and understanding of community.

The significance of etymology comes forward under Tom's eye, particularly as words have connected people with one another and nature. He reminds us and even directs us to work on and understand the common ground that a community can and must share if true culture is to emerge. Not an easy process in the hyper-cyber active world where face-to-face encounters are vanishing and the measure of the individual is too often what's in a bank account rather than an accounting of living in balance with one's ecosystem. Follow Jay's narrative quest for the deepest meaning of a word and wonder at our drift in priorities when we have minted and employ scores of words for money and only a handful of terms for moving water. His insights in an essay entitled "Familiar Music: Reinhabiting Language" is a challenging consideration of how the words we use, reflect the increasing separation of people from one another and their community.

What we face today, in matters of environmental degradation, depletion of natural resources and the fractious relationships between people and nations makes this book all the more important and timelier. It is a brilliant assemblage of thoughts and realities that opens up possibilities for personal priorities to restore our connections with nature that are critical to our future. These are first-hand, place-specific ideas, opinions and insights coming from an authentic individual. He's shared exquisite examples of the rewards that come from close and patient scrutiny, whether it be an object of art, a salmon, a bird's nest or a dragon fly. A reading adventure awaits you.

Tony Angell
Seattle, WA.
April 29 2019

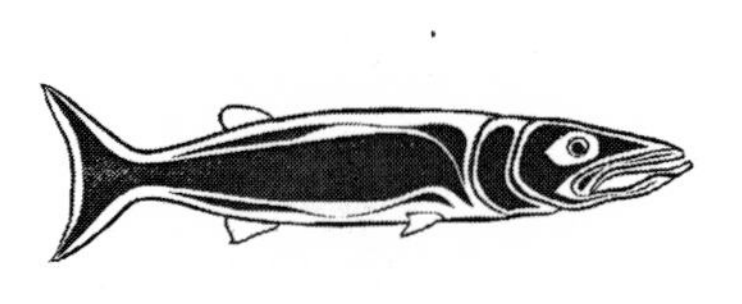

Finding Moving Water

I learned I could water witch from an old South Dakota farmer, Leonard Lechtenberg, who came to our green Western Washington valley after WWII to try dairy farming. I called him because he was recommended by my neighbors as a real dowser—he could find water. I called him up and asked if he would witch a well on our place. "I don't witch anymore. My heart isn't what it used to be, but come down to my place for a visit, and we'll find out if you can dowse. If you can, then you can witch your own well." Intrigued and skeptical, I accepted Leonard's offer and drove to his place to find out if I could dowse or water witch, whatever that meant. When I arrived, Leonard came out of his white clapboard farmhouse and waved at me to come up onto the porch. He was a black-haired gnomic man in his late sixties, stocky and almost plump, but powerful from years of hard work. He was naturally friendly, but not in a superficial way. From the beginning of our friendship, it was obvious that Leonard valued life's marrow more than its makeup.

After a brief chat and a survey of his farm and outbuildings from the porch, he invited me into the kitchen and produced a pair of 3/16" steel rods about 2 1/2' long, bent at right angles about six inches up their length. They looked like letter Ls. "These are witching rods. They're a great tool for finding veins of water if you're a dowser." He went on to explain that about one in four people can water witch to one degree or another. "It's like a birthmark, fingerprint, or the color of your eyes; you can't learn or will to have such gifts, you are born with them." He showed me how to hold the rods, parallel to each other, the legs of the Ls level with the ground, with the feet of the Ls held vertically in the socket of the fist so the toes of the feet point down. The socket of the grip allowed the rods to pivot when they were over or on a vein of water. "I prefer the steel rods," he said. "They tell you more. You can trace a vein or tell when you hit a crossing vein. Some dowsers prefer a forked green willow branch. The branch is shaped like a Y. You grip the end portion of each arm of the Y with your palms up and with the single leg of the Y parallel to the ground. When you strike a vein, the leg points down. It feels like you've got a big fish on a strong line." In my experience, it feels like an invisible hand stronger than your own two is pulling the willow tip down into the ground. Sometimes this invisible force is strong enough to twist off the bark in your grip, or snap the arms of the Y because they are over bent by the pull of the hidden stream—the vein, as Leonard liked to call it.

"Either way, willow or steel, if you're a real water witch, you can't stop them from moving no matter how hard you try. Remember, dowsing is finding veins of live water, moving water. It's not the water, it's the water's motion you feel in the willow or steel." With that introduction, Leonard took me out onto the front porch and pointed to the access road that ran between the house and the barn. "Hold the rods as I showed you, tight, but don't put your thumbs on top of them. If you're a dowser, the rods will cross in front of you at a certain point down the road."

I walked down the steps toward the road, and Leonard went back inside. When I reached the road, I paused to check my grip on the rods, and turned to see Leonard in the kitchen window, waving me on. "Just walk slowly down the road," he called. "There's nothing to get; you either have it, or you don't!" So off I went, tentative and awkward, with the rods a little shaky in my uncertain shuffle. I wanted it to work, but didn't know what it was, so I couldn't fake it, or even encourage it. I walked on slowly, half-afraid, half-hoping, foolish and expectant. About twelve summer-dusty paces toward the barn, the rods began to turn inward, inexorably, determinedly, magnetically. Fascinated, I resisted the pull, squeezing the rods as tightly as I could, but true to Leonard's word they ignored my strain and crossed in eerie benediction.

"I thought it might work for you!" Leonard yelled from the kitchen window.

"Amen," I muttered to myself as I hurried back to the house. "Wow, it works," I said and laughed.

"Yeah, you passed the test," Leonard chuckled. "The test?"

"Yes, some people want to fool with the rods to avoid embarrassment if they're not real dowsers. But I know from witching all over this place that the only moving water on this little road flows through a pipe buried right where you watched the rods cross. The pipe brings water from our well to the house."

"How did you know the water was moving?" I asked, still treading water in the little miracle welling up around me.

"While you were fiddling with your grip on the rods, I turned the sink water on. It's a foolproof test for would-be dowsers. Be careful, the rods pull strongly for you, so learn to temper your enthusiasm. You're not in charge, you're in touch."

Leonard then gave me a brief survey of folk learning around dowsing. He cautioned me to remain alert while witching and to check out willows and anthills in well-drained areas. Twenty-plus years of water witching have confirmed that folk learning. Ants and willows have a nearly unanimous predilection to locate their colonies and roots over veins of water. Science is only mildly curious about folklore, so I haven't uncovered any papers on ant or willow sensitivity to the electromagnetic dynamics of moving water. We do know that moving water is a "current" and creates a weak magnetic field by the motion of electrically charged water. Maybe the ants and willows have their own highly evolved dowsing abilities that help them locate and thrive over the veins that the rods reveal and wells confirm.

In his humble but telling remembrance of dowsing lore, Leonard mentioned that traditional peoples of northern Europe often kept a trout in their wells, in the belief that the water would be blessed with freshness. Science has recently discovered that pre-smolt salmon, fry and parr use the water-saturated, gravel-rich hyporrheic zone that flows next to, in and out of, and about rivers and streams. The young salmon swim freely in the interstices of the perennially dark gravel and probably feed in its unknown ecology. In the hyporrheic zone the fry and parr are safe from larger predators who are too large to fit through the doors of that dark haven. I mentioned this finding to Dick Goin, a long-time Olympic Peninsula salmon advocate and restoration volunteer. He said, "Oh yeah, I remember once we were digging gravel to supplement flood-scoured spawning beds. Our pit was at least twenty feet from the main channel and, you know, it wasn't long before we began to see young salmon that had followed the seep into our temporary gravel pit." It's not unlikely that European "well trout" were salmon fry that preferred the safe waters and easy food of the well to the chain mail gravel they used as refuge. No doubt many of them stayed too long and grew too large to slip through to the larger stream when the ocean called. They became well-locked salmon, virgin queens trapped in the upside-down drowned towers of the underworld of springs and spirits. Folkloric witness and scientific fact, the blossoms are ghosts at the wedding.

My research reveals that Celtic mythology celebrated sacred wells wherein the Salmon of Wisdom dwelled. Pre-Christian Ireland had numerous wells haunted by sacred trout or salmon until the Christian church re-blessed them all with saints' names, and they became outposts of an alien lord's grace, rather than the mysterious blood of the local earth, the milk of the ancient goddess of creation.

Leonard told me to practice witching known wells, "to refine your feel," he said. He explained *bobbing*, witching for depth. The technique requires the dowser to hold the end of a 5–6 foot steel or willow rod over the found vein and touch the bobbing rod to that spot, then lift the wand slowly until level with the ground, at which moment the rod will begin to *bob*: bouncing up and down over the vein. The dowser counts these bobs and uses the count to learn the depth of the well. By bobbing known wells, the water witch learns to calibrate his or her bob. My bob is a simple one-foot to the bob.

Leonard also showed me the rudiments of tracing a vein. Once the rods cross over a vein, you stand directly over that spot with the rods crossed, then, dropping your arms to your sides, you turn 90 degrees left or right and raise the rods, holding them parallel in front of you as before. If they stay parallel, you're in the flow and can trace the vein by walking slowly forward, watching the rods and changing direction to keep them parallel over the flow. You wobble slightly side to side as you follow the vein's meander beneath the earth's mute forms. You follow a vein for two reasons: maybe there is an easier place to drill, and perhaps you'll hit a cross vein, increasing chances for more well capacity. When you hit a cross vein, the rods will open outward as if in welcome. When you bob the cross vein, the bobbing wand will hitch and circle once or twice at the shallow vein before continuing the count to the deeper water. Whether you use the steel rods or supple forked willow, water witching works. At least three quarters of the several wells I've witched over the years have come in at the indicated spot and within seven feet of the bobbed depth. When the witching hasn't worked, either the well driller moved the rig off the spot, or more interestingly, the well log reveals gravelly or sandy substrate that once bore water, but is no longer wet. It seems rocks may remember water flow, who knows? Dowsing has nothing to do with my talents, intentions or intelligence; it is nothing to be proud of, but a gift to be grateful for, like fine sight or being able to sing in key.

Since that day on Leonard's road, the ground beneath my feet has become a different creature. A well is now a noun and a verb. It is no longer a hole in the earth to mine water. It is a reverberation, a window, a womb, a breast, a liquid locus of belonging where the wet, sun-stilled mystery of the world rises to refresh us. We are glints of light in the moon-knotted lace of water that ensouls the land. The blossoms are ghosts at the wedding.

Like writing, dowsing is a profound refreshment for me. Neither work nor play, it is a kind of serious dreaming proved finally at the point of a stone-tempered drill or ballpoint pen. Hydromancy is similar to poetry in that, like hidden, moving water, you have to risk and dig to enjoy its refreshment. You have to work slowly, attentively, to reveal whether the current's call is an inspiration or an illusion, a weak shallow vein or a potential artesian. Sometimes you're stumbling through a blackberry-cursed clear-cut and sometimes you're strolling in the shaded sanctity of an ancient forest. (It's no accident that speech is from an Indo-European root *sper* that gives us sprinkle, sparkle, sperm, among other wet familiars. Similarly, *rhyme* and *rhythm* spring from another Indo-European root *sreu*, to flow, which gives us stream and rheostat among others. The basic notion is current.) For more than twenty years I have witched the occasional well for friends and neighbors. I don't charge; few dowsers do. "How could you charge for the color of your eyes?" warned Leonard. Dowsing's traditional simple implements invite the ancient genius of our bodies' notions to trace the subtle snake of living water in the earth's heat-cracked, bone-littered heart. Likewise, the well-grounded living word and the subtle ancient echoes of daily conversation locate and instruct the poet's rainy inspiration.

The blossoms are ghosts at the wedding. Our world is haunted by water. But besides the stone-breaking insinuations the dowser divines, we are part of and prey to water's slippery pandemonium—in rills, frosts, fogs, seas, mists, waves, springs, clouds, aegirs, in tides, in blood and bodies, in lakes, ponds, floods and drenching rain. Water haunts life inside and out; we die without its grace. We are its clay-footed, star-eyed offspring, ocean's orphans upright in the wind. Our water-born awareness bends to the well-spoken word the way the willow branch twists and dives in my work-hardened hands. Both currents are real as rain. We have only the death-stirred crucible of our hearts to receive their vivid, whispered renewals. The water-mothered weather of this mortal world and the braided babble of songs and cries that edge and animate our mortal masks are the threads that spin our fate. The dowser's witness and a breathing poem are forms of pledge, an inner weather wherein the leaf-voiced wind runs ahead, alone and empty handed to announce the arrival of the soulful, salmon-eyed rain. The blossoms are ghosts at the wedding.

Initiation

Years ago I worked as a boat puller on a troller fishing the Fairweather grounds, west of Glacier Bay, Alaska. We were newcomers to Alaska. The skipper, Larry Scoville, was an old friend and seasoned Northern California troller. We were fishing a new boat with a new diesel, so Larry and I spent a few days in the fjords and passes around Elfin Cove rehearsing the gear, the boat and crew. We were testing FV *Sinara* for any quirky motions, vibrations or noises that might spook the wily salmon. Larry watched my side of the boat, counting the fish caught, and warned me if the salmon didn't like my smell I'd have to wear gloves when I baited leaders or changed "hoochy" lures. The *Sinara* worked, and I was confirmed a bare-handed boat puller. We caught a scatter of silvers and kings and headed for the Fairweather grounds and the chance to catch some big king salmon.

The second day on the grounds, Larry had us fishing frenetically on a school of stout king salmon. In the midst of the blood-slippery melee, Larry called me to bring the landing net to his side of the boat. He was working a tremendous king salmon on a rubber snubber we called the kill line, and gave me instructions on how to approach the salmon with the net, because it would have been foolish to land such a large salmon with a gaff. It was the biggest king I had seen that summer, slab-sided, thick-bodied and five feet long, perhaps a 100-pounder. As I brought the net behind and under it, it began to swim away not fast, but steadily, like a draft animal pulling a heavy load. The kill line went taut and the 100-pound test line snapped as the great fish flashed out of sight. This story is a reminder that the salmon is free and that the musings that follow are only lines and hooks that hold it momentarily.

The season was a bust. The silvers were late and the kings, hit or miss, so I quit before the season ended and went south to Seattle to study and work. It was seven years before I saw another free salmon. Settled with my family in the Olympic Peninsula community of Chimacum, Washington, one frosty winter evening I walked to the modest alder-lined creek that winds through the pasture south of our place. Lost in the icy stillness, I was startled by a sudden, staccato splashing. Whatever it was gathered its energy in quiet, then burst forward again, closer, moving up the creek. I crept to the cattle bridge to glimpse this night visitor.

In the ice-blue light of winter, a salmon flourished, dorsal fin and back just breaking the easy iridescent ripples of the stream. Another dark sparkling dash and it was below me in a log-dammed pool. It was a large, wild male coho, smoky red and silver in his spawning regalia. Migrating at night while hunters dream, the salmon had followed the scent of this creek home, a pilgrimage repeated faithfully by his ancestors since the last ice age.

Witnessing the homecoming of this ancient being, the salmon, so precise, practiced and generous in his longing, quickened my own sense of homecoming. I felt lost and found at the same time squinting into the polished darkness of the water, afraid to lose that timely guide. In that numinous moment on the bridge, salmon became my teacher. He has kindled and animated my curiosity and I have followed him into the haunted waters of watersheds and folklore. Since that night on the bridge, salmon have been swimming in my dreams.

Salmon are born in brooks, creeks, rills, the headwaters of greater streams. They run to the sea for a miraculous sojourn. Feasting, their flesh reddens in the richness of the sea. Mature, they awaken to the call of their natal waters, and follow clues subtle and disparate as magnetic fields and the bouquet of stones to the streams of their birth to spawn and die. Loving and dying in home ground is a primordial urge. Salmon embody this for us—our own loving deaths at home in the world. Salmon dwell in two places at once, in our hearts and in the waters, and they know the way home.

Once nearly every watershed around the North Pacific Rim, from San Diego, California to Kyushu Island in southern Japan, supported one or more runs of Pacific salmon (king, sockeye, pink, chum, coho, steelhead, masu, and amago). Each run or stock of salmon fits itself over eons to local conditions, its adaptability tempered by ice ages, floods and droughts. The vital beauty of salmon has been shaped by the infinite refinements of necessity. The salmon's genius is in making friends with fate. The king salmon of the Elwha River in Washington, for example, have evolved to enormous size, up to six feet and 100 pounds, because females must be powerful enough to excavate spawning beds (redds) below the scour depth of this steep and highly energized river.

The myriad life histories and the fine and grand morphological differences the salmon have evolved over thousands of years might be imagined as embodiments of watershed character—the salmon an expression, a vernacular of the watershed. Logically and poetically, the salmon are the soul of the watershed, its glory. Salmon are, as the salmon restoration herald, Freeman House, announced thirty years ago, the totem of the North Pacific Rim. Freeman was restating a wisdom familiar to the indigenous peoples of the North Pacific Rim. The Yurok of California and the Ainu of Japan, while separated by thousands of miles of ocean, celebrated the salmon as a vital element of their cosmos. In many regions human culture coevolved with the salmon, because both species—*Homo sapiens* and *Oncorhynchus*—were recolonizing the post-glacial barrens at the same time.

In the rub of weather and landscape, Native peoples and salmon adapted behaviors to fit local conditions. As the glaciers retreated, strays from refugia salmon populations began to probe the meltwater rivers and streams that drained the tundra landscapes of the glacial wake. Periodic heavy glacial outwash could wipe out generations of salmon and limit the success of salmon forays into new watersheds. While the persistent salmon fertilized the raw waters of glacial watersheds, plant communities, migrating north and south from unglaciated botanical preserves, were gradually reestablishing conifers in the post-glacial landscape. It was this "conspiracy" of salmon and trees that transformed and stabilized the watersheds of the North Pacific.

Large conifers provided shade, stream structure and a detritus-based aquatic food chain that nurtured the various species of Pacific salmon. Salmon runs moved tons of sediment downstream and helped stabilize river channels. Salmon also returned ocean-gathered nutrients to the rain-leached and glacially plowed soils of much of the North Pacific. As spawning and spawned-out salmon were retrieved from streams by bear, otter, eagle, raven and others, their nutrients were distributed throughout the forest.

A local forester once took me to a gargantuan grandmother fir, still regal in a mature second-growth forest. Four large people holding hands could barely encircle its girth. Its wind-blasted top was crowned with an active osprey nest. While we all craned our necks to view the nest, the forester pointed to the foot of the tree and asked what we saw. Around the base of the tree were tracks and scat of all kinds: coyote, raccoon, bear, deer, squirrel. "You see," he said, "the young osprey are much like our children when they dump their oatmeal off the high chair, except here the dropped food (salmon) is mopped up by a host of creatures, even deer and squirrel, who nibble the bones for calcium." This great fir, miles from any salmon creek, was a distribution point for forest nutrients. By dropping salmon from the treetops, the osprey were providing a welcome feast for the savvy creatures below. Seen in this light, salmon are a current between the forest and the sea. Salmon are sea-bright silver shuttles weaving the rain-green world of the temperate Pacific watersheds.

About 5,000 years ago, when salmon were established and abundant, Native peoples would move seasonally to fishing camps along streams and feast. But when the runs were over, the people had to move on after other food, for they had yet to develop food preservation techniques to take full advantage of the salmon bounty. Once Native peoples mastered salmon food preservation, they settled in permanent villages near preferred fishing sites. They learned through over-harvest and calamity-induced famine to manage the salmon resource at maximum sustainable yield. Pre-contact native cultures were probably harvesting more salmon than nineteenth- and twentieth-century industrial fisheries. Some researchers estimate that the Native harvest of salmon in the Pacific Northwest had been reduced ninefold before the large influx of European pioneers. The thundering "walk-across" runs reported by early European settlers were likely the result of tribal populations being decimated by the epidemics and whiskey that announced European eminence.

In pre-contact times, by working diligently during the salmon season, a family could store in a few months enough fish to meet its basic food requirements for a year. Of course there were supplemental foods—deer, seal, whale, fowl, shellfish and plants, berries and seaweed—but the fundamental food resource was salmon. It was the axis of their economy and the hub of their culture. The salmon's abundance gave early peoples leisure, the time to develop the refined and distinct cultures of the North Pacific Coast.

Given their long association with salmon and its importance to them, it is no wonder that original peoples developed a deep and coherent connection to salmon. We moderns love salmon; it is the choice food of our region. But to the first peoples of the North Pacific, salmon was not merely food, it was energy. It was not energy in our sense of BTUs or calories, but was what William Blake meant when he said energy is eternal delight. Native peoples' close relations with salmon had worn through to a kind of intuitive essence: the salmon was the animate representative of greater powers, a fellow being and fateful herald of an *aweful* universe.

Many peoples of the North Pacific honored the salmon on its yearly return home. They imagined salmon as a representative of the other side, the world where the powers of creation reside. To the Ainu, Gilyak and Chukchi of Northeast Asia, the salmon was representative of the sea spirit. To the tribes of the Northwest Coast, it was a supernatural human being whose village was in the sea and who put on the salmon disguise as a gift to honor the respect the local people showed the salmon people.

In the Native cosmos, salmon can choose to present themselves in abundance or not at all. This vision required special treatment for the salmon. When the S'Klallam of Beecher Bay, British Columbia, caught the first sockeye salmon, little children sprinkled their hair with sacred white eagle down, painted their faces and put on white blankets. They met the canoe and carried the first salmon in their arms as if it were an infant. An older woman cleaned the fish with a mussel-shell knife, after which the flesh was boiled and given to the children to eat. To the S'Klallam, the sockeye is a person and deserves careful treatment. Versions of the first salmon ceremony were practiced by Native peoples from California to Japan. The salmon was treated as a respected guest before it was eaten, so that when the salmon spirits returned to their watery villages they would report that their gifts had been honorably received.

For the first people of the North Pacific, the salmon was a gift from hidden but prescient powers. The salmon was sacramental food, and the proper attitude was to feast on its energy in gratitude and repay its generosity by respectful treatment. You couldn't have your cake unless you ate it in gratitude. The Chukchi of Kamchatka ate the first salmon caught themselves; they wouldn't sell it to their Russian masters. You can't have your cake and sell it, too. The Gilyak of Sakhalin Island, north of Hokkaido, Japan, had a special language for speaking to salmon and other game. The Koryak of Siberia had a story called "Fish Woman" in which a man marries a fish woman, and though she is loving and patient, the mistreatment she receives in his house causes her to leave and take her relatives with her. This story echoes a Northwest Coast Tsimshian tale wherein a man mistreats his wife, "Salmon Woman," who returns to the sea with her silvery familiars. Native relations with the salmon resource required the same care, responsibility and attention as marriage, all qualities crucial to survival.

In the autumn, the Ainu of Japan watched for the magnolia leaves to fall because this presaged the arrival of the chum salmon. When they took the first salmon from the river, they passed it through a special game window in their house and honored the salmon ritually in front of the hearth fire. In their world, fire could see and report back to the supernatural world the hospitable treatment of the salmon. The Ainu also had a ceremony to bid the salmon spirits farewell when, in their human form, they paddled their canoes back to their homes in the supernatural world.

These beliefs are a deep recognition and affirmation of the place of the human imagination in nature. Native legend is a well-spoken alchemy of soul and landscape, each story informed by a thousand tellings. The wisdom of Native peoples is to live in and husband a world wherein nature and its beings hold humans responsible for their actions.

I once swam down Washington's Duckabush River in wet suit and mask. It was during the dog salmon run and there was a flood of fish in the river. The current ran both ways that day. Halfway down the river I floated over a deep pool where an eddy had piled a pyramid of golden alder leaves. Further on, resting in the shallows and musing on what I'd seen, I noticed a shape move behind a submerged snag. It was a large male dog salmon, splotchy gray and yellow with faint copper tiger stripes; spawned out but alive in his eyes. I dove and glided toward him until we were a foot apart. I looked into his eye. He saw me but did not move. I was just another river shadow, an aspect of his dying. He was crossing over to the other side, watershed specter feeding the firs, subterranean sometime king, tree-born elder, tutor.

Familiar Music: Reinhabiting Language

My father, Layton Leroy Jay, was a miner in his youth. He worked in the lead and silver mines of northern Utah. He "mucked" and shoveled his way through college, a year in the mines, a year in school. He could still outlast me with a shovel well into his sixties. My father was proud of his hard-won education and encouraged a large and practiced vocabulary as proof of its discipline. Whenever I had a question about word usage, he sent me to the giant anvil of a Webster's that doubled as a flower press in the corner of our living room. It was a proud day for me when I could finally carry it to the privacy of my room. From our first encounter the dictionary was a source of wonder and reverie for me. In its cogent dream I discovered that language is a vital reality and that each word preserves and expresses a perception, a subtly consecrated and traditional moment in the articulate mystery we call life.

Language called me like a secret ally from a forest's shade and I found myself a fledgling sparrow in its weathered wealth. I read the dictionary for pleasure, marveling at the depth, nuance and diversity of the language I spoke. I studied Latin because it amplified and inflected many of the words we breathe into English each day. Language is still numinous territory for me and perusing a well-conceived dictionary is like sneaking into a darkened, ancient church and daydreaming in its rainbowed holy shade. But it wasn't until my thirties that my calling to language was confirmed by a startling lexical epiphany.

I was thirty-six years old, an egotistic, almost young poet whose first poems had been published a few years earlier. Still hungry for praise, I was trying to write poems, force poems, establish a reputation. But inspiration had abandoned me, evaporating like the fey glimmer of a tree in summer mist. The poems soured, became tacky constructs of sentiment, murky perception and waning wit. The poems were loud, Hawaiian shirts of poems without a hint of the silence that frames and sustains an original poem. I hadn't learned that poems are not made; they're born and raised, like orphans left crying at your door.

> *Original* inherits its verbal means from Latin *origo* ("source, spring"). The root image in *original* is water rising out of the earth, water struck from stone.

One spring day, confused and parched in the untimely drought of my dilemma, surrounded by crumpled scraps of paper, I confronted my language romance with this complaint: "Okay. These poems are pretentious and contrived, muse-less; so if the muse is real, tell me her name." I waited attentively in the wisp of my innocence, pen in hand, expectant. But no answer arrived and after a while spring's green spell subverted my vigil and I began to doodle and daydream, absent-minded in the verdant charm of the day.

I woke from my reverie an hour later and there among the florid mazes, architectural cartoons and fantastic geometry of my doodles was a single word scribbled unawares: *kuma*... off I went to my trust of dictionaries. *Kuma*. I looked for her in three sources—no help. Still a persistent voice watered my hope, "Maybe you spelled it wrong. Maybe kuma is an old word." So I tried again and found it under *cyme* in *Partridge's Origins* (a short etymological dictionary of modern English.) A *cyme* is an inflorescence, a young cabbage sprout, the decoration atop a Greek column. *Cyme*'s root is Greek Kuma, ("a wave, a sprout, anything swollen"). Kuma is from the Greek verb *Kuein* ("to be pregnant"). I had my answer. One fair name for the muse is *Kuma*, a swollen wave, a sprout, a form generated in the great dream of the somnambulant sea, headed your way, headed my way. She announces herself with a whispered roar and breaks radiantly on our peculiar shores. Since that spring day I seriously attend any word or phrase that wells up in my mind.

That daydream taught me that one had only to absent the personal mind as agent, yet maintain it as disciplined witness, and the deep intelligence of language might emerge. In that moment I learned the truth of the muse: that inspired language, spoken or written, originates not in personal cleverness but in the fertility of language itself. The uncanny surprises in the realm of language—"Freudian" slips, unexpected eloquence, hot-cross puns and poems born fully grown and dancing—are the natural blossoming of language's richness, the dark prescient wisdom of its ancient and mortally tested soul. The essential Eros of language is evident in the way we name the details of our daily work. The logger keeps an eye out for a widow maker, a loose and potentially dangerous branch perched in the tree he's felling. The salmon troller arranges her "hoochies"—luminous, googly-eyed imitation squid—neatly by the hydraulic gurdies she works so deftly, bouncing her heavy lead on the sea bottom, luring king salmon to strike. Language's vitality metaphors the world it attends. It is the spoken music of our animate, many-weathered and deep-soiled home.

About that time I became curious as to the nature of my local community and began to study ecology. Kuma's revelation that language is inherently and naturally alive resounded deeply with ecology's essential metaphors: community, co-evolution, locality and cycles. I began to imagine language as an ecology, as vivid and nuanced as a forest. I came to see English as an atmosphere, a climate, the deft, rich warp and weft of human witness. Language is a locale, a temporal location and soulful place wherein we make love, dream and die. We wrap ourselves in the familiar roll of its weather, we are its water.

> *Ecology* from Greek *oikos* ("home, dwelling place") and *logos* ("talking, logic, legend"), hence *ecology* ("the home story, home legend, home logic").

A notable concept in ecology is the notion of the edge. When two ecosystems meet, say the forest and prairie, a border of rich diversity and fertility precipitates between them, a place of increased imagination. The evolved, well-practiced narratives—*oikos* ("stories")—of the two systems are mixed in a terminus, a verge of opportunity and peril. Our ancestors probably became bipedal and brainy in the fertile shift of the tropical forest and savannah verge. In function and practice language is more truly an edge ecology, a fertile border, a vibrant brood between the human soul and the natural world.

Language is metaphoric. It bears our attention beyond ourselves towards the world. In speech we meet and affirm the gritty mystery of being, and in that affirmation, language is a lively marriage of soul and cosmos. Language is naturally erotic, a nearly forgotten form of love, the caress of shaped breath. Denied its connection, its Eros, we wither in the alienated self-reflection of jargons. I see language as the spoken record of myriad meetings between humans and the cosmos, two natures woven into wisdom, a fertile border, a skin with soul on either side, a semi-permeable membrane, a go-between, a Janus-headed Robin Hood, mercurial, tricky and true, inside out a glove that fits either hand...weird old words.

Language has a life of its own, and words, contrary to contemporary percepts, are not so much tools as organisms, evolved symbiots living in the breathed edge between our psyches and creation. Rather than sharpening, oiling and polishing our terms we do better to respect our words as if they were plants and animals; attend their generosity and wisdom rather than manipulate their resource. We might re-imagine ourselves as hunter-gatherers in the ecology of language rather than as engineers, mechanics or arrogant tinkers of its raw material. Words are more like game trails than machetes. Our word *term* once meant “border”. A term is where we meet the world. The spoken or written word is the articulation of that meeting, the I-Thou joinery, its joint. Speaking and listening well allows insight to the informed silence of the other side, becomes a room where the other may enter. Language is the habitat of revelation, yet language will lie if forced to do our bidding. But if we honor its lore, the lasting track of its vitality, it will invite us to speak. *Speak* shares an Indo-European root, *sphareg* (“to swell, teem, abound”) with (“spark, spore, sprinkle, sparkle, disperse, sperm”). Language is a fertile liquid.

But language not only sparks and spores, is not only a seminal presence; it is also a soil, an archaeology, a ghostly host to its own story. Calvin Watkins, a noted philologist, was able to reimagine and locate a creditable homeland for our Indo-European ancestors by simply listing the oldest root words in the Indo-European family of language and cross-referencing the list with the findings of paleo-ecology in Eurasia. The list included root words for *bear, mouse, hornet, beech tree, salmon* and others and tentatively placed our ancestral home west of the Urals and north of the Black Sea in the ancient forest that covered what is now Eastern Russia. Languages evolve, adapt and borrow; words have lineages and genealogies. Linguists can deconstruct a modern term and identify its ancestor word and the period when it began its haunt of the habitat we call English.

Every language on the planet has an age. English is relatively young, almost nine hundred years old, the child of a spear-point wedding between Norman French and Anglo-Saxon. Some languages are thousands of years old: Irish, German,

Greek, and Persian. Some are tens of thousands of years old: Kung, Ainu, Basque and the Aboriginal languages of Australia and the Americas.

Each language has been lorically shaped by its home-scape. Languages live and die, lasting as long as their lore is true. According to the linguist Michael Krause, minority languages in the English-language sphere face a 90 percent extinction rate between now and sometime in the next century.

> *Loric*—from Old English Laeran ("to teach, to lead someone on their way"). *Laeran* is akin to Old English *Laest* ("track"), which gives us *last* ("what endures, a remaining way, a path that lasts"). Lore is a lasting, well-worn track, the way of the ancestors, where your foot touches the ground.

"Therefore, in these days when a major problem is the growth of an originally Anglo-American, but now genuine global, monoculture that reduces everything to the level of the most mind-numbing stupendous boredom, I would think that the preservation of minority languages like Irish, with their unique and unrepeatable ways of looking at the world, would be as important for human beings as the preservation of the remaining tropical rainforest is for biological diversity." Diversity is the wealth of eco-systems and culture, the wealth that time and life have heaped upon our shore, cumulative, Kuma again, gracing the shore of our awareness.

> *Articulation* shares the Latin root *artus* ("joint with art, arthritis, artificial") and ("inert not-jointed"), hence ("unable to move").

Languages offer unique perspectives on the world, different articulations of reality. Twenty years ago I had a conversation with a young friend named Ben. When Ben was five or six years old his family moved to the South Pacific island of Woleai. His parents had contracted to teach English as a second language to the people of Woleai. Ben soon became fluent in Woleain and entered the culture it centered. For eight years Ben spoke English with his parents and Woleain with everyone else. I once asked him if he believed in ghosts. "When I speak English, I don't," he replied. "What do you mean?" I asked. "Well," he answered, "When I speak Woleain on Woleai I see them." Language in synch with a landscape ripe with ancestral mythology quickens a cultured, shared reality where the storied richness of the past animates and accents the present moment.

The Irish poetess, Nuala Ni Dhomhnaill, makes a similar point. "Irish is a language of enormous elasticity and emotional sensitivity; of quick hilarious banter and a welter of references both historical and mythological; it is an instrument of imaginative depth and scope, which has been tempered by the community for generations until it can pick up and sing out every hint of emotional modulation that can occur between people. Many international scholars rhapsodize that this speech of ragged peasants seems always on the point of bursting into poetry."*

Further on she picks up the theme on a deeper level. "The way so-called depth psychologists go on about the subconscious nowadays you'd swear they had invented it, or at the very least stumbled on to a ghostly and ghastly continent whence mankind had previously never set foot. Even the dogs in the street in West Kerry know that the 'otherworld' exists, and that to be in and out of it constantly is the most natural thing in the world. The easy interaction with the imaginary means that you don't have to have a raving psychotic breakdown to enter the 'otherworld.' The deep sense in the language that something exists beyond the ego envelope is pleasant and reassuring, but it is also a great source of linguistic and imaginative playfulness, even on the most ordinary and banal of occasions."

Lewis Thomas was right when he commented in the final pages of *Lives of a Cell* that perhaps our central purpose as human beings is to ferry language and its myriad manifestations into the future. We are all bees in the honeyed hive of language.

The diversity of languages, like the diversity of species, is founded in landscapes; mountains, rivers, seas and deserts impound and amplify our various linguistic streams. After the collapse of imperial Rome, the Pyrenees and Alps isolated Latin speakers into provincial dialects that evolved into Spanish, French and Italian. The ethno-linguistic puzzle of Aboriginal California is nearly synchronous with the larger features of Californian geography. Long residency in a locale, dwelling in its *focus*, works resonance into language; local vernacular, the precious "mettle" of neighborhoods, is coined in the slow alchemy of humans rooted in place.

> *Focus*—Latin for *hearth* ("the dwelling place of the household gods").

The deep wisdom and prescient witness of languages rooted and nourished in landscape seem archaic to modernity and its current shibboleth, the sharp-toothed "wisdom" of the market. It is telling that the defining metaphor of recent society, "the bottom line," derives from a business profit and loss statement. Evidently our reality is founded on currency, cash flow and liquidity. No wonder our endeavors seem to float and drift rather than root or stand. Money and the easy logic of profit have conspired with hyper-inventive technologies to foster a civilization addicted to speed and change, revolution rather than evolution. The fossil-fueled mechanics and spendthrift energetics of modern civilization and its entropic friction with the natural world have serious consequences for the conservative dynamics of language. Market-induced entropy has overwhelmed and obliterated indigenous dia-lects, witness the Amazon, and demeans our present speech into a creature of advertisement rather than eloquence. But business and the market are not identical. The market is a mercurial roil of appetite, ambition and opportunity. Business and labor are the boat and crew that ride its weather. The heart of the market is profit, but the traditional heart of business is trade, relationship. Business crafts and trades often speak vividly of their endeavors. Investment originally meant to clothe.

Certainly language is not static. Words are born and die; like other life forms they adapt their behaviors to fit new circumstances, new weather. Words may spiral through a classical, almost formal, transformation from an original meaning to its opposite. The pilgrimage takes around three hundred years. C.S. Lewis, in *Studies in Words*, followed the word *sad* through its peregrinations, documenting its turns with wry insight and wit.

In Chaucer's time *sad* meant full, the way you feel after a large meal, drowsy on the couch after Christmas dinner. *Sad* as full, can—by a small metaphoric stretch—also mean heavy. So it wasn't long before *sad* implied weight, heft. Further on in its gyre *sad* as weighty or full became *sad* as solid, firm, sound; "heavy" as we said in the sixties. Then *sad* as solid came to describe human character. A man or woman of solid character was *sad*. *Sad* applied to persons of dignity and quality; elders, tested and tempered, were full *sad*. But character can age into gravity and severity and it's not far from the grave and serious sense of sad to our present sense of *sad* as tristesse or melancholy. *Sad*'s pilgrimage reflects our changing perception of the elderly but its journey is also revealing because although *sad* shifted its attention as it traveled through time, it never lost its root sense of fullness (sated!) The bloom of the word changed color and shape in the slow roll of human weather but its roots were firm. *Sad*'s journey happened in what we might call natural time, an evolution confirmed by small changes. But times have changed. For the last 150–200 years English has switched its "watch" from natural time to commercial time. Natural time is grounded in cycles, the blooms, tides and seasons of human beings on the earth. In the quicksilver reality of global markets and modern technics, landscape is irrelevant. In money's abstract reality the map is the territory! I remember talking with a corporate forester who sadly remarked that accountants who couldn't tell a hemlock from a Douglas fir now managed timber harvest.

Words fare no better than souls or small birds in the reductive heat of commercial-industrial time. Consider the word *bad*. *Bad* has recently somersaulted through our speech, its gyre a circus act rather than a stately shadowy round dance, a revolution rather than an evolution. When I was a child in the late forties and early fifties, *bad* meant wicked, a sense still close to its root meaning of "open to all influence especially the worst." By the time I was in high school, *bad* still meant *wicked* to my parents but to my peers and me it meant brazen, tough, strong and fearsome. By the seventies, Michael Jackson had promoted *bad* into a term that evoked daring and personal power. *Bad* nearly finished its loop in thirty years. I fear for *bad*; we may have exhausted it, fried it in the overheated rush of our impotent ennui-driven need for clever new twists of speech to advertise our "attitude."

In the turbulent flux of our diversions, words are disappearing as fast as Amazonian song birds in a clear-cut, not to mention the degrading effects of recent commercial efforts to mine the language resource to produce new hybrid words, word alloys to smooth the skid road of commerce. Think of the car names or the titles of perfumes or the pop monikers of breakfast cereals and toilet paper—Accura, Obsession, Turbo, Kix,

Downy—soulless words, unredeemed, vacant-eyed hustles, toxic schemes swept along in the fertile river of our gab. The artificial hybridization and kidnapping of words by commercial hype tends to thin and poison the character of our speech; slang on the other hand tends to renew it. I regret that there is not room in this essay to delve into the yeasty role slang and the jagged edge of underworld vernaculars play in "rapping," inflecting, inspecting, infecting and deflecting the pretensions of mainstream culture. The underworld with its pimps, carnies, shills, bums, burlesques, whores, crooks, tramps, junkies, punks and sharks—with its smothered ethnicity and twisted ambition—has been fertilizing English since its quickening with the Norman arrow in good King Harold's eye. Slang lives in the shadows of conventional speech, inventive, quick, predatory, afraid, feared, ignored and hence subversive. Slang mocks our conventions and by its bravado helps the language turn. Imagine a sinister, half-starved jester whispering into the fat right ear of the sleeping king, napping on a Lear jet bound for tomorrow.

Notwithstanding the underworld's best efforts, students of English report that English is losing its spoken vocabulary, the diversity of its *terms*, despite its eminence as the lingua franca of the planet. And therein lies the reason for its malaise. Perhaps English is forfeiting its descriptive power because it has assumed a generic monocultural perspective. Still, there remain spirited English vernaculars, dialects of local color and weather-quickened wit. (I recall my West Texas brother-in-law's description of Ross Perot as a hand grenade with a bad haircut.) But the neighborhoods of these loric idioms are increasingly vulnerable to the acetone commercial media and its "solvent" capacity to smudge the subtlest and brightest hues of lingo. It is diffcult indeed for indigenous beings— birds, words, plants, critters and perhaps now even weather—to escape the money driven institutionalized revolution embodied in modern growth capitalism. But permanent revolution—cultural, economic or political—is terror as real as Robespierre's, Stalin's, Khomeni's or Mao's. We are conspiring with that terror in the way we've let ourselves be named. We are now by consensus and our own calling *consumers*. The word consumer derives from a Latin word *consumo* ("to spend everything, to destroy utterly, to destroy by fire").

> *Market* from Latin *merc* ("merchandise"), hence ("commerce, mercy [the price of pity?]") and ("Mercury, god of trade, speedy messenger") and ("secret thief ") and lastly ("guide to souls to the otherworld").

In a kind of delusional apologetics we now equate consumption with citizenship. But as late as eighty years ago *consumer* had negative connotations. We used the term to name a selfish and wanton sort. The change in the word's usage testifies to a changed society. Eighty years ago we called ourselves neighbors, citizens, and brothers and sisters, kith and kin. Neighbor is an Old English word which meant near fellow dweller. Citizen is from an Indo-European root *ci* or *cei* ("to lie down, to rest"), the same root gives us ("home" and cemetery"); a citizen is a homebody, a deep dreamer. Kith and kin arrive via Old English *cyth* ("native land"), and *cynn* ("kindred, one's own kind"), hence *kith* and *kin* ("the local haunt").

Like any living creature English wants to know where it is; where we have ferried it now...it isn't Sherwood Forest. Now spoken English surely lives with commerce having become estranged from local culture and the places that engender it.

> *Culture* from Latin *colere* ("to turn, to till the earth"). The poetry in "culture" is implicit. The soil is the past, the ancestors. Practicing culture we turn the ancestors into the light so they may bloom and nourish us. Culture is soil born.

English presently has more words in its spoken vocabulary for money than it does for moving water: bread, bucks, dough, change, cash, whip-out (my favorite), long green, swag, roll, stash, dibs, currency, quid, pile, jingle, lucre, pelf and plastic are only the skim of a longer list that doesn't include technical terms for money and monetary transactions. These words describe specific and nuanced relations to money; whip-out is not a term favored by investment bankers, nor is pelf or lucre likely to leap into the hipster's rap. English is faithfully articulating our reality, firming and confirming the current edge between us and the larger world. The rub is that our world by the witness of our words is becoming a fantasy, the placeless, neighborless realm of modern commerce.

In contrast consider these words that name places and things that unspoken may be unnoticed: *lea* ("a meadow drenched in sunlight"); *rill* ("a small forceful stream"); *lynn* ("a pool beneath a waterfall"); *beck* ("a small brook") and *brook* ("a break-out in the bank of a larger stream that waters a marsh") and lastly *kelt* ("a spawned-out salmon or hung-over reveler). Speaking these words may re-articulate and re-enliven our world. The Northwest poet William Stafford said, "Sometimes a poem is writ to let one word breathe." The true genius of English, its poetic eye and musical ear, the subtle temper of its humor, is reticent, musing in the hinterlands "out of touch," waiting out the scourge of money's reductive fire, faithfully naming and calling the winds, rains, and creatures of the neighborhood, the kith and kin of the natural world forsaken by its mother tongue.

In the early sixties two bioregional visionaries, Freeman House and Jeremiah Gorsline, used Peter Berg's term "reinhabitation" to describe a social antidote to the devastation of natural and human communities by economies of transient consumerism. They proposed that the most revolutionary act was to settle permanently in a place and assume responsibility for the neighborhood with all the near fellow dwellers, mountains, rivers, flora and fauna and, I might add, English. We must reinhabit our language as well as our ecologies. If we stay put in deed and word our selfish rap will gradually unravel and in time re-weave us deeper into place; our speech will become part of the texture of locality, its felt meaning. Then our reality might once again resound with ancestral echoes and the myriad voices of the weather and the land. Our words will become again the welcome and the witness of our home's peculiar beauty and our lore will last nurtured in the practiced cycles of locality.

Imagine your home-place: the giant oak in the park, the bandstand with the leaky roof, the white ice-scoured mountains, the evergreen forests and thigh-thick winter steelhead, the polished stone of your father's grave. Imagine the familiar surround and the horizon of words that hold your world as the rim of a bell. Imagine you are the tongue of that bell, silent and still in its shelter. The tongue cannot will itself to move and ring the bell, only the swollen wave of weather's mystery may move tongue and bell together and ring out familiar music.

* Nuala Ni Dhomhnaill, "Why I Choose to Write in Irish, The Corpse That Sits Up and Talks Back." January 8, 1995, *New York Times Book Review*.

There Is No Art for Art's Sake: The Blossoms are Ghosts at The Wedding

Forty years ago I witnessed the casting of bronze sculpture. Perhaps it was the Vulcanic river of metal or the fragile bone-white molds, but the pour converted me and I began a lifetime relationship with art and artists. Bronze casting for sculptors has been a fruitful and educational association. Each new work requires detailed physical consideration of the piece, its nature and how best to translate it into metal. These considerations are usually practical, dealing with the material, logistic and structural aspects of translation of images from one material to another. There is always some private or shared reflection on the nature of the piece: what it wants to be. Philosophical musings are not foremost in my work but they do haunt, enliven, curse and bless it. I realize that although I know when a *piece* is "art," I can't always explain my perception. Perhaps it is because art has become an all-inclusive and hence blurry term. It no longer deepens our experience or vitalizes our understanding. We only vaguely know what we mean when we say art. Few dare ask, "What is art?"

The word *art* sprouts from the Indo-European root word *ar* or *er* ("to fit together"). The root generates words to describe joints, joinery and joining of all kinds. *Art*'s verbal family includes arm (the related limb?), article, articulate, armature, and *inert* ("ill fitted, ill-jointed, unable to move"); *inert* is *art*'s opposite, ("inart"). Other cognates are arithmetic, arthritis, ratio, reason, read, ritual and harmony. All these words are haunted and enlivened by the root notion, *ar* ("fitted together"). Ritual is a fit with the gods. Reason is fitting things or ideas together. Ratio is a mathematical description of fit. Harmony is the tone of a fit. *Artus* in Latin was also the male member, the joint. Art *is* seminal, the fit is lively.

Art is a fitting together, a well-made joint, an articulation, the way the bones in your fingers work together, or words in a Yeats poem, or an osprey's wings in a light wind. Art is a primal and ancient form of connection. The first art object may have been "discovered" by a *homo habilis* person 400,000 years ago. This ancestor of *homo sapiens* who had fire and probably language found a hand-sized, round stone that appeared to have eyes. Was the stone "looking" or "seeing," who knows? We do know that the eyes were not made by human hands; they were naturally occurring depressions in the "face" of the stone. We also know that the stone was an object of veneration because it was purposely stained with red ochre to mark it as sacred, to acknowledge special connection with "the stone with eyes."

Before the superficial, speed-fed blur of modern media, art traditionally articulated our world, weaving imagination into local context, knotting the treads of our experience into meaning, re-presenting it in sacred light. In shrines, songs, dances, bells, drama and lore, it cadenced our mortal vitality, shadowing it with beauty. Art's joining and jointing is not mechanical or reductive. Art is not a circus contraption. It is an invitation to belong to creation, to share and acknowledge its endeavor. It is crafting the fit of inspiration and material that is the creative act. Inspiration and material are gifts and art doesn't belong to the artist, he belongs to it.

Art's joinery, its "fitting together" is *metaphoric* from Greek *meta* ("beyond") and pherein ("to carry, to bear"), hence, our metaphor "to carry beyond"—imagination and practiced perception rowing the boar of surprise. Art is metaphoric craft that ferries us beyond ourselves. The inspired artist transforms his medium into a nexus, a crossroads of material and mystery, a landmark of wonder, a well to quench our thirst, a focused stillness, an oddly familiar room to attend the whisper behind the curtained door. Art is a way-point in life's stumbling bruise of amazement, the evening path in the forest, an intimate human-trod edge with unknowing "familiar mystery." The artist midwifes our way into the startling weather of the secret world. Art's "articulations" encourage us, give us heart to listen to the other, to welcome the guest who shows the way.

We should remember that, while etymologies deepen our sense of art's "work," they may also demean art's larger mission of transformation and communication. If we were to curse it with an exclusive etymological ball and chain, we reduce it to clever joinery. Art's works, its articulations, are often paradoxical and chimeric, even magical, revealing by concealing, a silk cloak thrown on a fickle breeze. Art is not merely telling, it is also the alchemical coaxing of matter's shy soul into clear witness. Art is not a trick; it is a trickle, a spring of unknown source that quenches our thirst and the cup that lets you drink.

Traditionally the artist's work pivoted on, and was informed by, his materials. They located and centered his inspiration. The material was the *medium*, the body that let the ghost of his inspiration live. Our word material derives from a Latin word *materia* ("timber, wood"), and by extension, other materials, "stuff" we use. *Materia* came from the Latin word *mater* ("the hard part of a tree, the trunk that produced shoots"). This *mater* is a transferred use of *mater* ("mother"). *Mater* comes from the Indo-European root *ma* ("breast"). *Mater* is the "nourisher." When you cut down *mater* you get *materia*, hence, our *material* ("the dead mother"). In pre-Christian Europe the great mother goddess was all-powerful and ubiquitous. Her milk ran in streams and issued forth in springs. Rhea was the mother of the gods; her name meant to flow.

Maybe artists and their intimacy with "materials" are secretly coaxing Rhea's bounty, inviting it to well up through our simple monuments and quench the fire-parched thirst of the fathers. Art is digging for water with a word. There is no art for art's sake; the blossoms are ghosts at the wedding. No wonder we knock on wood for luck.

Land, Earth, Soil, Dirt: Some Notes Towards a Sense of Place

Years ago, the morning after an evening of beer drinking and poetry reciting, a hungover clot of revelers was walking back from breakfast. Northwest poet Robert Sund, whom I had met the night before, lagged behind the rest of us, preoccupied. He had stopped and was staring into a corner, a crack where two concrete buildings met. Curious, we went back; he looked up from a small, cranial-shaped pile of moss and said something like, "That's our only hope." We laughed nervously, a little shaken, it struck us all. The moss was patiently turning the buildings to soil, to dirt, to earth. That moment has haunted me since, and the idea of soil and its import has become a recurrent meditation for me.

I want to look at soil as a metaphor, as a self-darkened lens that bends light, dividing, revealing, obscuring; a lens to watch light thickened green by life and kneaded rich by death's dark hands. I want to behold a rainbow as the faint echo of soil's gravid hive. Imagine soil as the context, the textural background of other imaginations, an other, darker nature grounding culture, personality, language. A good place to start is in the words we use about soil. By examining, exhuming, the stories hidden in them, we reveal a strata of unconscious attitudes towards soil. We say "back to the land," "mother earth," "good ground," "dirty," but only vaguely know what we're saying. Our descriptions lack discrimination, want felt meaning. Reviewing the stories biding in the words and following their instruction, we may resuscitate a poetic, a way of seeing and knowing the local world we walk upon.

Land is a word nearly synonymous with soil. We cultivate, plow and till the land. But these are activities originally germane to soil. Their use with land is an example of the natural poetic license that dwells in language. Land is from the Indo-European root *lendh* ("open land"). This sense still adheres to the cognates of *lendh*. Old English has *land* meaning specifically ("open land"). French has *lande* ("heath, moorland, especially infertile moorland"). Our word *lawn* comes to us from French *lande*. Old Slavic has *ledo* ("wasteland").

German has additionally *landau* ("water meadow") (land + *owa* [water]). Old Celtic has *landa* ("a valley"). Welsh and Cornish have *lann* ("an enclosure"). *Land* is a relatively abstract term that refers to boundaries. Its basic idea is open or closed space. Its root does not refer to any other specific aspect of landscape except its openness or closedness. At heart, it's about "land shape," about surface, not soil.

Land's meaning for us is *owned topography*. The idea of property is the word's current context. To express other qualities of landscape requires qualification: heart land, forest land. Land no longer constellates an image. We can "land" anywhere. There is a land romance: some of us went "back to the land." But it is telling that we went back to the land (an abstraction) not to the Palouse, the Olympic Rain Forest, or even the heath, desert or forest. Part of the diffculty of the back-to-the-land movement is that its speech does not adequately inform its impulse. For us land is a concept, not a locality.

Earth is another word we substitute for *soil*. It is a word with a surprising spectrum of meanings. Its root is the Indo-European *er* ("earth, anciently and essentially the place between the heavens and the land of the dead"). It is the name of our planet, Earth, gravity's burrow, the invisible genius that keeps our feet on the ground and tethers moons swole scythe-like magic. Gravity, whose pull prescribes and consecrates our orbit and allows our blue-green, fire-hearted dream to dance its tragic dance around a dying star.

We cannot yet "buy earth"—we find that hard to say. Historically, earth has meant or still means: the world, cosmos, soil, surface, country, chemical oxide, the place between heaven and hell, electrical ground (British), a grave, a burrow, a shelter. To condense all these meanings we might say earth is the place of fundamental, fateful connection.

Dirt is the unsavory side of our descriptions of soil. *Dirt* is from Old Norse *drit* ("excrement"). *Drit* is from Old Norse *drita* ("to shit"). It is telling that we use a word with that root to describe soil. Healthy soil digests shit and puts it to use, but dirt and soil are not the same. Granted, soil can be dangerous if fouled by poisons or diseased wastes, but we are missing the fundamental difference between soil and dirt when we confuse them. Soil is a "community enterprise." Shit is potential nutrients "looking for work." We do *dirt* dirty, using it as a synonym for soil or earth. We should maintain its specific connections to excrement. Earth and soil are not shit. An earthy mind and dirty mind are different gatherings. I wonder if there isn't a ruling class prejudice hiding in the continued confusion of dirt and soil. It's almost as if the soil were beneath us instead of holding us up.

Ground is another word associated with soil. Ground is from Old English *grund* ("foundation, earth"). *Ground* means bottom; a "groundling" was originally a name for a fish that lived on the bottom of ponds or a person who preferred, or could only afford, the pit in front of the stage. *Ground* means fundamental, basic. We run aground; we are well grounded in thought. Many disciplines use the word (carpentry, naval terminology, philosophy, engineering, art, etc.). Ground is cognate with Old English *grynde* ("abyss"). So, ground is cousin to depth and mystery. It is also used in reference to soil and landscape. We work the ground, the groin, also from *grynde* ("abyss") of the earth. Perhaps we confuse soil and ground because soil grounds us, soil is *fundamental*; it *grounds* us. It completes the circuit.

Finally we come to soil, "the root metaphor," "our only hope." Soil is the secret sublimation of the land. It is the black, alchemic gold of this green earth, the re-enchantment of waste and death. It is the humming dignity of the gravid ground, the black honey of our sun-drenched hive. Soil is an earthy, grounding term that is not land. Soil is not easily owned or domesticated. It suffers our earthly antics with motherly patience calmly awaiting our return. Soil's history as a term is fascinating. In time it has meant: a wild boar mire, a pool of water used as a refuge by hunted deer, sexual intercourse, composition of the ground, mold, staining, to purge a horse on green feed.

Etymologically, soil has two roots. First, soil is from Indo-European *su* ("to produce young"). Cognate words are sow, succulent, socket, hyena and hog. Pigs were sacred to the earth goddess. Pigs and snakes were her favored images. The sense that comes to us from this root is mire or stain, but behind these senses—"in the roots wild pigs are breeding and birthing at the mired edge of ancient oak forests; deer are dying near a hidden pool." "Soiled" we touch the sacred suckling succulent sow.

Soil's other sense (ground-earth) comes to us from Latin *solum* ("ground floor, threshing floor") and the obsolete ("solium, throne"). The Indo-European root is *sed* ("to sit, to settle"). Soil's cognates are nest, nestle, seat, soot, cathedral, sole. Soil is where we stand. The "soles" of our feet touch the soil, grounding us. "He's got his feet on the ground." Soil is a throne of bones where light nests, where we settle. The ancestors tickle our feet from its fertile shade.

Soil is a kind of bicameral word. Like a good two-house legislature, it "converses." The two root meanings, *fertility* and *seat*, have intertwined since Middle French, when the words became identical in sound and spelling. Indeed the sow is enthroned in soil. Soil is the throne, the nest that bears young, the queen' s room. Soil is the land in hand, smelled and seen. Soil supports the living and receives the dead.

The science of ecology affirms the etymological complexity of soil. From *Ecology and Field Biology* by Robert Leo Smith: "Soil is the site where nutrient elements are brought into biological circulation by mineral weathering. It also harbors the bacteria that incorporate atmospheric nitrogen into the soil. Roots occupy a considerable portion of the soil. They serve to tie the vegetation to the soil and to pump water and its dissolved minerals to other parts of the plant for photosynthesis and other biochemical processes—vegetation in turn influences soil development, its chemical and physical properties and organic matter content. *Thus soil acts as a 'sort of pathway' between the organic and mineral worlds.*"

In short, soil is the bridge between the living and the dead, both in one, a living death, a paradox. Geologist Robert Curry explains the crucial connection between soil and human life: "All (forms of) life, without exception, are dependent upon outside sources of nutrients for their support within a substrate upon which they nurture themselves. In all non-marine systems, the ultimate substrate is soil. Even marine systems are dependent upon weathered minerals derived by soil-forming processes throughout geologic time on land. Soil is not an inert inorganic blanket of varying thickness on the land that can be differentiated into subsoil and topsoil. Those naive terms belie a basic misunderstanding that permeates the agricultural advisory services of this country. Soil is generally recognized by soil scientists to be a dynamic, living assemblage of precisely bio-geochemically segregated macro- and micronutrient ions held in a series of remarkable storage sites. These nutrients are provided by slow weathering over geologic time and are translocated and reprocessed by soil organisms and plant activity. In general the living biomass beneath the ground equals or exceeds that above ground.[!]

"Soil is thus not a mineral, geologic resource but a biospheric resource that, although renewable, can reform only at extremely slow geologic rates of tens of centuries. The soil nutrients within their delicately segregated geochemical levels represent precisely and literally the sum total of the long sustainable economic capital of the nation."

To paraphrase Curry, we might say soil is fate. This notion resonates with soil's connections to seats of power, the sow goddess, soil our destiny, our destination. Soil is the land in hand, a specific place. Soil embodies the meeting, is the meat of weather and rock; "remembers" them into trees and kingfishers, salamanders and salal. Each location knots that meeting differently. Your county soil survey becomes a kind of earth phrenology—soil is a live being, a dark leaf breathing water and light. Soil is myriad neural serpents writhing knotted on an infinity of their discarded skins. It is its own renewable research, a porcine cannibal lover, phoenix, shit-eating alchemist, Ouroboros enshrined, an honest mother. Persephone, goddess of spring lives underground, ensoiled. She rises in spring, wife of wise Hades, King of Wealth and Death. Her name means "bringer of destruction." Perhaps she is a personification of soil, the living death. Demeter's virginal daughter married to the king of the dead. (Interestingly, in one of his myriad seductions, Zeus, the king of heaven, approached Persephone in the guise of a snake as she sat in the great cave of creation weaving the threads of destiny.) Plants and animals follow her back into the light. Soil blurs the distinction between the living and the dead, humbling us. Soil is the pious Confucian son tending the graves of the ancestors. It is husband and wife in one dark body. Soil is the dwelling wave, the archetypal, renewable resource. *Resource* from *re-surge* ("to surge back"), and *surge* is from Latin *sub-regere* ("to rule from below"). So, a resource surges back ruled by powers hidden from view. Soil is the paradoxical death-dark well of our living. Soil is the resurrecting, hidden ruler, fate-maker, dark-eyed, blossom-giddy girl weaving destiny deep in the ground.

We are all earth-born, literally and figuratively, and the word *human* confirms this assertion. Our words human, humble and homage all derive from Latin *humus* ("earth, soil, ground, region, country"). A human is earth-born, shares the quality of humus. It is well to remember that to our ancestors humus was local and that "humanity" was born, arose from a specific locale, a place. The people over the hill might not be quite human, in the sense of your local humus. Our language knows we are earth-born even if we think we are heaven sent.

Human awareness is the blossom in the fertile mix of two soils, the soil of language and the soil of place. The "soil" of language is not merely metaphoric, it is mortally real. Language wants a place, a locus, as much as you or I. Vernaculars are living proof of languages rooting and blooming where it lands. Language grows into where it lives, symbiotic; old world metaphors re-sown into new landscapes. Our perceptions and our witness catch the stark light and green it into meaning. These meanings compost and compose a deeper experience of where we are. Words are living beings; they borrow our breath for inspiration; they blossom, fruit, root and die.

Language in place, ensoiled, inevitably blooms culture. Culture in root means to plow, return, cycle. Understood etymologically, culture is soil homage. Culture grows out of and dies back into language in place; the stories enrich the words. Culture is the sacred blossom; it consecrates the ground, soul and soil of the same dark being.

Western society has abandoned the older notion of culture, the husbanding of human life in place. Our culture does not arrive through the discrimination of the different songs the wind rings in the several pines of the Sierra, or the terror of the child lost in the rain forest, or the shape of a fisherman's pipe; no, instead we buy our culture. It is a consumer item, an *uncouth* import.

Whether it was dire necessity or some fatal species-specific flaw, we took to the wind with a cross and sword. We learned to grow anywhere, choke out the natives. (Aboriginal peoples often die of homesickness.) We came to favor shallow roots, learned to grow in places we wasted. This may be what we really are, but our language once lived in a neighborhood where the word for tree and truth were the same—Indo-European *dru*, whence ("truth, tree, trust, druid", etc.) Each speech has an accent, the odor of composted history. If left alone, our patterns of speech become localized, "dried" by the heat, made pungent by rain. But our electric neighborhood ignores locality; dialogue is now electrified. Blind as a volt, our tongues are in the radared air, groundless. TV is our tree.

The soil is where we return our dead; it is the home of the ancestors. This sense of soil is lacking for most of us. We are careless. I have not witnessed the lives and deaths of my kin. True to the American dream, we scattered, seeking private versions of wealth, ignoring Hades' dark treasure. I am less for my lack of witness. Human life grows in weight and intensity as people stay in one place. The ancestors form a wedge behind us, press us forward on the edge of that weight. Depending on our ability to bear the weight, to balance it, our located word is good and drives deeper into the haunt of home or it breaks and we float up into the vapid torrent of commercial culture. Without the ancestors, without the soil of souls, we are potted plants, doomed in real weather. When we speak of living here, we should remember that perhaps the most important thing we will do here is die here, that our deaths will matter and be the first step in steadying our children's steps. Our graves will anchor them while they work the subtle weather of this cedar-green world. Soil supports the living and receives the dead.

Tilth

Tilth comes from Old English *tilian* ("to work hard for, to cultivate"), with associated words in Dutch, Celtic and German that mean opportunity, agreeable and pleasant. To till is to work hard, to strive for the good and agreeable. Tilth, then, is the quality of carefully tended and worked soil, a term that belongs to the farm and ancient soil of our speech. If we stay put long enough we might some day say of a good story teller, "Her words have tilth."

Beacon

The first time I saw a woman naked I was six years old and it was the spring of 1949 in St. George, Utah. The winter garden had been dug up and the beanpoles set in the dark red dirt. I was playing hide and seek with my cousin Wally and in the middle of our chase I called time out and flew into my grandmother's white clapboard house to pee. I burst into the bathroom without knocking and there was grandma Jen, just stepped out of the shower.

Her gray-streaked auburn hair was loose and down to her waist. She had a shower cap in her hand and was reaching for a towel. Time stopped for me. Her face, neck and arms were a ruddy tan from years spent hiking in the high desert sun. But her nakedness was a creamy, lightly freckled, plump robustness. She was a big-boned Scots woman who could work with the men. But it was her breasts that held me in stunned fascination, beckoning me not in an overtly sexual way but in an awakening, fateful way, the mysterious invitation and promise of otherness. She was at that moment its emissary. Every man knows, though few admit, that women are the crucible of our character; that a woman traditionally frames and invites a man's fate. Grandma Jen was a bounteous Venus who, for a few stunned seconds, revealed a mystery that still beckons. Then she spoke in a calm and dignified voice while she reached unpanicked for a large towel, "Tom, you'll have to wait outside while I dry off and dress. I'll be out in a few minutes." Her voice brought me to my senses and I suddenly felt dizzy from the scent of lavender soap and stumbled out the door.

Later that visit grandma Jen took me hiking to the top of a mountainous white rock the locals called Sugar Loaf. It was higher than I'd ever been before. She asked if I'd like to peer over the edge. I said yes in a kid's unknowing, slightly fearful way. She wisely took my hand and as we reached the edge vertigo, inspiration or madness grabbed me and I stepped out into the deadly drop below the rock. Intuitively grandma Jen caught my fatal momentum on the first step and swung me in a quick arc over the void. We walked away from the edge and she said in a quiet, reassuring way, “Let’s creep up to the edge this time and see what we can see.” We did and I don’t know if she noticed or not because she was kneeling behind me and had her hand around my belt; but there one hundred feet down, was a ledge and a dead fawn, two ravens pecking at its eyes. I didn’t say anything and neither did she. My world changed forever.

On Mountaintops We Are Starkly Soulful

I first saw Mount Rainier in the early sixties. I was hitchhiking back to college in Southern California after a spring visit to a friend at the University of Washington. The weather was overcast and a restless mist masked the Cascades. I was facing north on Highway 99 thumbing the remnant morning commute when the sky cleared, and I didn't see "the mountain" until I turned south to walk out of the midmorning traffc backwater. And Rainier was *there*, looming shockingly huge, an inscrutable giant, hoary preadamite elder, above the dim cacophony of the strip.

Suddenly and incontrovertibly imminent, the foreboding eminence of the earth awoke in imagination, a mysterious, faintly ominous majesty, a monument honoring a force beyond my ken, a presence both familiar and strange. In that brief startled blink, Rainier seemed like the fire-darkened crown of eternity.

In the origin myths of traditional culture, a mountain embodies the archetypal beginning. The mountain is the center of the world, the navel of the cosmos. Mythologically, the mountain rises from the primal chaos of waters, marking and clarifying the murky horizon of ocean and sky. It separates the first mother and father and arrives as the first child of eternity, centering the sea, lifting up the heavens.

The mountain was the first earthly home, a place for the gods to play and the fellowship of creation to thrive. The first temples imitated mountains. The ziggurats and pyramids were sacred because they were mountain-like. At the top of the temple, at the top of the mountain, we were at the center of the earth, the place where time begins.

The montane inspiration of early temples is true. The few times I have been on mountaintops, the exhilaration I felt was not from being "elevated" or closer to heaven but from something less grand yet more fundamental. On summits, knolls, tumuli, promontories and peaks, we are most pointedly aware of our peculiar human situation, face in the cloud-scoured heavens, feet firm on rock rooted deep in the hot-hearted gravity of the planet. On mountaintops we are starkly soulful, grounded in the ancient earth, quickened in the oblivion of the sky, simple wind-shivered lightning rods of wonder.

Mountains are the bones of the Northwest bios, the essential architecture of its salmon-haunted dream. Imagine the Puget Sound climate without the Cascades to thicken, funnel, dam and direct the wet marine weather of our latitude. Imagine our lively, unpredictable rivers without the gravitational force the Cascade cordillera supplies. Imagine our salmon-rich streams without the rattling braid of water-rounded gravel that issues from the steady wreckage of the mountain slopes.

Mountains inform all life here, are the bone of its animate body, the firmness of its character. Rainier, "the mountain" in Puget Sound vernacular, symbolizes the mountain's elemental role in the Northwest drama. "The mountain" is the regent, the lava-hearted monarch of this wet green eddy of creation.

But Rainier is not merely royalty. My spring-sudden epiphany of Rainier's eminence, ineffable above the toy-like intensity and commercial anonymity of the American highway, has ripened in long reverie into something darker and more fertile than I have allowed so far.

Our word *mountain* is rooted in the Indo-European etymon *men* ("to jut out, project"). This root gives us the Latin word *mons, montis*, hence our word mountain. The same root *men* supplies the Latin verb *minari* ("to project, overhang, to threaten") and arrives in our speech as *menace*.

This etymological coincidence echoes an intuition that beneath its stately repose, its unfathomably dense and weighty "jut," Rainier is dangerous. "The mountain" periodically swells with mercurial fire; storms pivot on its prominence and many people have died in its crevasses, blizzards and avalanches. Rainier is dramatic and beautiful because in our hearts it is edged in a shadowy sublimation of peril. "The mountain" is a slow-motion Tsunami of fire, rock and ice; one day it will break and blow us away. We secretly fear it the way we fear God. The mountain inspires awe and dread. We are a mountain-fearing people.

But the mountain sublimates more than our fear. The ancient Irish imagined prominent hills or mountains as "sidhes." A sidhe was the fairy abode, the place where the perennial spirits of the land abide. For me, Rainier has become a sidhe—the dwelling-place of the forgotten spirits, the fateful energies of life in the Northwest: raven the changer, cannibal woman, salmon woman, snot boy, thunderbird, the throng of personae who spoke through and for the life here and who hide now in the mountain's dome awaiting re-invitation into our desiccate commercial culture. In my imagination, Rainier shelters their natural sovereignty.

The mountain that still startles us is a fundament, a temple, the first place, a terrible power, a sidhe, the secret hive of our children's dreams.

Larva

In summertime we swim in our neighbor's lake. Sometimes after work in the early fall when the water's too cold for Dru or Sara Mall, I go back to refresh myself.

About twenty yards out from the dock that we dive from is an old fir snag, riddled with woodpecker holes and home for the perennial alder who sprouts, grows a few years in the rotting bark, then dies. It is the place mosquito larvae crawl out of the water to begin their eerie gelatinous transformations. It is a totem, a vertical shore, and I swim to it instinctively each time I enter the dark lake.

My ritual is to swim to the sunward side and inspect the trunk around the waterline to see what's new. One day as I hung still in the cold water of the snag shade, an osprey passed just above my head: I felt the wind of its wings—from above, a wet head of dark hair must look like a fish bloated by the sun. It's good practice to imagine one's head as food.

But the most marvelous thing that ever happened at the swimming tree was, like many transformations, small and took a long time to happen. It was late afternoon in August; I had swum to the snag and begun my perusal of its trunk when I noticed, about a hand's width above the water surface, a strange, armored, insect-like creature clinging to the bark. It was the size of a small double-nutted peanut and still wet from its rise out of the lake.

Its shape reminded me of a Hudson Hornet with thirteen coats of amber lacquer, Kerouac's favorite car, a shape you might drive south or in a dream. The last Hudson Hornet I had seen was driven by a saintly Macedonian bouzouki player in L.A. It reminded me of moth pupae I sometimes unearth in the garden, and I remembered that *pupa* is a verbal familiar of the *pupil* in schools and eyes. It was a larva of some kind. Writing this, I discover *larva* was originally a Latin word for ghost or household god. Seeing it there on the bark brought back the times I tossed a log on the fire and watched a spider running the wrong way up its length. The larva was numinous as the pecking noise inside an egg. It was baby Osiris wrapped in an amber shroud.

It rested there in the setting sun, drying off. It amazed me how anything could be so still. Then in an instant its eyes lost the light and a hump bulged up on its back like a child balling up beneath its blankets in nightmare. The hump began to pulse like a fouled sail or hammered thumb, then suddenly burst and out slid what appeared to be a thin pearlescent phallus with eyes. It rested, half-emerged from its former body, now broken and dull, the light already haunting it; and I thought of the bouzouki player's deathless laugh as he drove out of the dingy gas station where I spent my youth. The creature was catching its breath, what the Greeks called *psyche*. It was calling old grandfather wind to enter it. He came and soon the newcomer moved, its whole body hearty as it left the wreckage of its water life.

It crawled a little farther up the snag, following the setting sunlight. On its back were two tiny veined balloons like water wings filled with iridescent fluid. Seen closely, they were like world maps drawn by some mushroom-eating medieval cleric. With each pulse of its newfound breath the balloons stretched a little and its body darkened infinitesimally to blue. It was pumping up its wings; it was becoming a dragonfly.

My body began to numb from the cold lake, but I could not leave. The silver was peeling off the back of my mind's mirror and the wind eye was opening, the world was winking at me. The dragonfly followed the sun up the snag. It was a desperate race; tree shadows crossed its path like the hand of God, a deadly cold welled up in every shade. Once about two feet up the trunk a large wolf spider jumped out at him—ambushed, I thought, a pilgrim with his throat cut—but the dragonfly rose up like an unhorsed knight, opened its forelegs wide in embrace as if to say, "Welcome home, sucker." The spider wisely retreated to its lair to prey again, and the dragonfly resumed its race with the sun.

At a long arm's length out of the lake it finished its wings and waved them resolutely in the evening air. I could hear their faint hum like a mother lullabying a child in a far room. If night had overtaken it, the dragonfly would have awakened in the morning a wingless hawk in a land of wolves, a dud, Babe Ruth with a rubber bat. I wanted it to fly: the mind's glass clouded again with silver, I was seeing myself again and I blew what was left of my warmth towards it. Twice-born, it knew better and folded its wings to await the sun's return.

In that moment and in my memory the dragonfly is *beautiful*, beauty being the marriage of freedom and necessity. It is the *promise* hidden in the form of a stone ax head, an old bell, a salmon, or a sorrowful song. It is what the ancients called Soul.

Red Boat/Pink Buoy

For Caroline and Dorik

In this fist of dark mountains, in the mercurial shimmer of this eternal yet transient curl of sea floats a red dory, tethered to the bobbing salmon-pink knob of an anchor buoy. The leashed boat cavorts and jibes with an animate dignity, like a well-bred horse or dog, spirited, gracefully testing its master's strength. The clownish noggin of the buoy holds its place with comic tenacity; a barely souled machine, a maritime R2-D2, the plastic apprentice of a sorcerer long gone enacting the koaned, tattooed directions.

"Hold the boat."

It is such an eerie pleasure to watch them play, the buoy and the boat. They practice a manifold carousel of emotions, the genteel peevery of the captive dory so eager for the sea, its patient frustration with its idiot groom. Sometimes, absentminded, they feign escape in a concerted tideward rush but are forever reined in short by the humorless unseen anchor and its bedrock instruction.

This pantomime, the tug-of-war burlesque, masks a deeper shade of mystery. Perhaps the pale egg of the buoy, a ghostly salmon egg, is tending Taliesin's sea-worn cradle* that teeters on the small tumulus of watery shadow beneath its lapstrake ribs. And what is hidden beneath the night-blue shroud of the dodging craft? Cases of rum? A set of hand-carved oars, brand new or worn smooth by the glassy oaken labor of rowing? Perhaps it is only the tangled Gordian knot of last year's fishing gear, a halibut-stirred mess of hoochies, hooks and lures. At sunset I imagine the boat a blood-red coffin sacred with the smiling mummy of an old Finnish fisherman, earth-brown pipe broken in his hands, the mutual clay crumbling at rest on the heavy breath of the sea.

My quixotic friends practice their soulful play "night and day" below my window, a faith that quickens my own dark, blood-slick dreaming. By my witness I have learned what they play. These alluring puppets of the sea rehearse the winds and tides that tempt us all.

11/95
Sitka
Margaret Calvin's Print Cabin

* Taliesin was the shaman/bard of ancient Wales, who was found as a babe, cradle lodged in a salmon weir. It is said his cradle floated 40 years at sea before his "arrival."

Words Bear Nature's Wisdom

As a child I dreamed of finding a message in a bottle. It never happened but later I found a phrase in my thoughts that satisfied my childhood fantasy. The phrase floated up on the shore of my mind: "Words bear nature's wisdom." It was a message from the hinterlands of language, from the background of our speech. So I searched the dictionaries, the accounts of travelers in that ancient land. I studied their versions and attempted this essay, a verbal sketch of the land the message came from. Actually these speculations are field notes, life histories of a few of the local inhabitants. Imagine the words reviewed here as plants or creatures living in a place called English.

When two ecosystems meet, say the forest and the prairie, you often see a border of rich diversity and fertility; a place of increased *imagination*. The metaphor of the fertile border informs this speculation. I'm imagining language as a spoken border that bends the light of the world into our shade, *informing* that energy until what we say is what we see. This is an admittedly romantic notion. In the "real world" language has become a narcissistic tyrant, a tool to keep the burning world at bay. Words make things real when it should be the other way around; *things* make our words real. Modern messages arrive in words; we are converted in conversation, not alone on the road to Damascus. Increasingly we experience the world as a simplified verbal conception avoiding its plasticity, its heat, its color and chaos except as they approach us through words. We have turned the words themselves, once gates for the world light to enter through, into guards to ward off the world. We blind the world with words and feel guilty that our contact with the cosmos is not more direct, more sincere. We suffocate in our speech; it becomes prophylactic rather than seminal. Perhaps because language is a human event we feel that it is cultural rather than natural. But language is not ours anymore than the estuary is the land's or the sea's.

Language is the fertile border. The world is in the words as we are. It's only because we don't listen closely enough that the world seems outside our speech. The world is in the words as we are; language is really a form of *introduction*—from Latin *introducer* ("to lead into the circle or house"), one echo-system to the other. Maybe words are message bearers who've been there and back, tricksters who see both sides at once; inside out, one glove fits either hand. A word is a meeting place, a shelter in the woods, a *tryst*, a *trust*, a *truth*.

I see language as the record of myriad meetings between humans and the cosmos, two "natures" woven into wisdom, a fertile border, an echo-system, the meat of our nature's meeting, a skin with soul on either side, a semi-permeable membrane, a go-between, mercurial, tricky and true. Language has a life of its own and words, contrary to popular contemporary metaphor, are not so much tools as organisms, evolved symbiots living in the ripe edge between nature and ourselves. Rather than oiling, polishing and sharpening our terms, we would do better to feed and water our words as if they were plants and animals, attend them, cultivate them, honor them, leave them be. We might approach them as hunters and gardeners rather than engineers, mechanics or arrogant tinkers. And if words are sometimes tools, then we do well to see the *life* in the tool, the wood in its handle, the bone in its blade. Words are more like game trails than machetes. The word *term* originally meant boundary. A *term* is where we meet the world. Speaking and listening well allows us access to the *informed* silence of the other side.

It's a sorry thing, but words are more often printed and read than *spoken*. We've taken words out of our mouths. The urban landscape is a riot of aestheticized print; super-graphics, billboards, neon signs, etc., while our speech resigns itself to pale formulae of grunts and trendy catch words. Our rap becomes our wrapper: the world a product, the wrappers disposable, the product consumed. We read in silence refusing the words' breath. It is only recently we took to reading in silence. St. Augustine was more frightened than surprised by his teacher who read in silence...and now we have speed reading, passing the words so fast they blur into a wall, polish into a mirror where we witness our alienation. But the world shines in the *inspired*, in the breathed, word. If we speak and listen well the world appears in the words. For instance, researching the history of words associated with books we uncover a marvelous series of vegetative images stored in the etymons. *Etymon*'s literal meaning is "true word" and etymology is "talk about the true word." The *etymons* are the roots the words grow from, the place where the stories of the *terms* are stored, meetings remembered.

For example the word "book" is from Old English bece ("the beech tree"). The first books were runic beech rods. A book's pages rustle like leaves. We leaf through a book. A page was originally a trellis, words on a page like leaves on a trellis. The word library comes from the root word *lubh* that means ("leaf or tree bark"). *Script* and *writing* grow from roots meaning to scratch on bark. Trees still sway in our *terms*, old forests haunt our speech. *Speak* itself is rooted in the Indo-European etymon *sphareg* ("to sprout, to strew, to scatter"), whence our words: sparkle, sprinkle, sprout, sperm and speak. These terms are cognate, "born together," born of a common ancestor like species of finches The kinship of these *terms* image words as wet burning seeds, breath-born sprouts twisting in the light.

I see etymology as a kind of divination, a revelation of the image, the meeting recorded in the heart of the word. Record is from *re-cord*, Latin for back to heart, hence memory. A recorder is one who takes things to heart, a minstrel, a singer who played a "recorder" that didn't use tape. Leafing through Eric Partridge's *Orgins*, the *Oxford English Dictionary* or the *American Heritage Dictionary*, we cultivate the images alive in the words we speak and read. *Read* by the way is kin to *riddle*. Because English is so modern, so smooth a tongue, the roots slide by our speech. The root images don't echo in our words. In older, less polished, languages the roots reverberate in the words; puns glisten like dark stones breaking the surface of the spoken stream. Our speech has become a blade we polish but never plow with. Our speech becomes self-reflective and vain rather than a weather-fated flowering in ancestral soil. Etymology places the word with its parent image. It makes our speech more familiar, more resonant. By the word roots we come to *terms*, the border, hear the word's heartbeat recorded. In the roots of words we are at the edge, the fertile border where words bear nature's wisdom.

Language is an ecosystem; words bloom from ancient roots. We taste them on our tongues, re-inspire them with our breath. I imagine them as old beings reborn daily walking on thin air like thistledown, reminding us words are communal coals rekindled by our breath, blooms cajoled from roots by changing weather. Words can die like whales, calypso orchids or elk. What kills words? What chases them away? What finds them? Do we starve some words and nurture others? Domesticate some while others return to the wilds of the unconscious? Game trails become freeways, Roman highways become ghost-ridden goat paths. Are the Gods that the ancients saw in words really dead, or awaiting rebirth, mouth to mouth recitation, the shroud unrapped? In Latin *mater* was a venerated mother-tree. Cut down it became *materia*, whence ("material, a dead tree, lumber"). Is a materialist one who worships the dead mother?

When we miss the roots we mistake language, making up words in our heads. *News Week-ese*, Nixonese, corporate double tongue, cyber-systems gabble and psychobabble are some recent examples. True words bloom from roots, the wild roots inside/outside A false word has no echo, no resonance, no answer, no ecosystem, no family, no ghost. False words are stillborn, born without hearts and hence unable to *record*.

I like the idea of words as *persons*. *Person* is from the Latin *persona* ("mask"). In Roman theater the players wore masks that the sound, their voices, came through; *per* ("through)" plus *sona* ("sound") gives *persona*, the mask the speakers wore. Words are masks the sound comes through, persons like us. Imagine them as persons, their spelled bodies traveling through time, changing costumes (customs) in tune with the weather. Each word a pilgrim with a venerable image, a talisman close to her heart. Each word bearing a bit of nature's wisdom, seeking true sight, inspiration; the breeze that whistles through the mask, rustles in the trees.

At the border we meet the truth; ourselves and the world resolved in a word, *true*. In the heart of truth there is a tree. Truth is from the Indo-European root *deru* or *dru* ("oak or tree"). Truth's cognates are truce, trust, tryst (now a lover's rendezvous but originally it meant waiting for game in the trees), durable, dryad, and druid. A druid is one who sees the tree. Partridge says the "truth is firm and straight as a tree." But ecologists can tell you there is more to a tree than firmness and straightness. *Trees* and *truth* are alive. (Life is from a root meaning sticky or sap-like.) A tree eats light, locks that energy in carbon and water, and stores the mysterious food in the roots. In fall a tree sheds its leaves to the ground where various organisms compost (de-compose and re-compose) them into soil, *humus*. *Humus* is the root for human, humble, humility. The tree nourishes itself on its death. The tree cycles all this energy, *informing* it. Roots feed leaves in spring; leaves breathe in light and CO2 to feed the roots and breathe out the air that *inspires* us. The roots pull minerals, broken stones, old bones, the bodies of all that dies nearby to build the tree. The heart of the tree is dead. The tallest tree is supported by its dying. Only its skin, leaves and roots are alive; its core is no longer sticky. Imagine forests of gray-skinned sadhus climbing their deaths to reach the light. In these ways a tree stores and restores its place. Maybe the truth is like that, a specific living mix of water, light and death. Perhaps philosophers should imagine themselves as orchardists or foresters or renegade loggers as well as architects of thoughtful edifices.

There are many trees, many truths in the human heart: *Yggradsil*, the world tree of Norse mythology had leaves in heaven, roots in hell. Yggradsil held the world together; in its shade lived the Norns, whose name means "whisperer." The Norns spin fates. Fate is from a Latin word *fari* ("to speak"). *Fate* is kin to *speech*, "coming to terms," and words as we shall see are spinners. Odin, the father of the Gods, sacrificed himself on Yggradsil. Osiris was imagined as a cedar tree. Gilgamesh destroyed the sacred forest and cursed his life. Genesis has its trees. In the *Rig Veda* the world is hewn from a tree by a cosmic carpenter. Every culture has its holy trees. Buddha found enlightenment beneath a tree, and Christ was crucified on a kind of tree.

The truth is like a tree and so is language. Language imagines itself as a tree. In dictionaries we see the "tree" of language: the Indo-European trunk branching into Balto-Slavic, Persian, Italic, Celtic, Germanic, and off these branches sprout smaller branches—Frisian, Breton, Rumanian, Latvian, Urdu—and each smaller branch is beleafed with words and rooted in a special place. The whole tree shimmers in the wind, whispering. Words have roots and stems, speech is sprouting.

Trees compose the soil, bear the air. Language grounds us, inspires us.

Perhaps language is a fateful tree—the leaves of our present speech absorb the light, feed the ancient roots that store the condensed images, the aeons of human weather, the rings. The health of the tree depends on the ability of the leaves to bear the light energy to the roots and the power of the roots to pull nutrients from the earth. Lastly the fruit, the bon mot, the poem, epics, the local joke, songs, new versions; the tree releafed again and again, turned to the weather, mendicant oak. The tree makes our world; we live in its shade.

Words bear nature's wisdom. Tracing the roots of this expression we re-emerge in other names, penetrate familiar images (*penetration* from Latin, *penes*, [inside]), blossom in other sprouts, verbiage, sparking words re-inspired, old wind in the world ash, laughter of ancient women gossiping over their drop spindles.

> WORD:
> Words are sources (from *surge*) of power, condensed myth (from *muthos*; speech, story).If you know someone's name, their myth, you have power over them or at least special access to them. Words were messengers of fate long before the Freudian slip. (A slip is also a twig or shoot; "a slip of a girl"; it also means to clothe, we slip into something, sleeve, sloop, slop, slope.) Is a Freudian slip stepping on a banana peel dropped from the weird sister's picnic basket?

When we delve into the root of *word* we come to the obvious; it is from the Indo-European root *wer* ("to speak"). But philologists offer no informing image for *wer* except to hint it may belong to a large tribe of words informed by a sense of turning and spinning. So *word* is a blossom close to the ground. When we say "words bear nature's wisdom" we mean what is spoken bears nature's wisdom. A word is one knot in the language web that echoes and re-imagines nature's complexity. From the turning and rolling in the heart of culture, to the race and running in current and course, every word is a metaphor using images to create nuanced connective meaning. The metaphor is firmed in our saying, and it is here that a clue appears that may reveal the way a word works. Saying and seeing seem to be etymological familiars; witness the similarity between the past tense *saw* ("having seen") and the noun *saw* ("a story"). Both share similar roots, Indo-European *sek* ("to say") and *sekw* ("to know"). The saying lets us see and viceversa. Likewise the root of *diction* and a host of other speaking words come from the Indo-European root *deik* ("to point or show"). A word, it seems, is breath informed with witness; the seeing spun into saying, the sage reciting the revealing saga.

Words are an echoic web, a silk-ragged lace vibrant in a world woven by wind, rain and light; our spidery minds so nimble on its ancient net, the breathy braille of the mystery we weave, the paradoxical see-saw-saying of living. Words bear nature's wisdom.

BEAR:
Bear means to carry, to endure, to birth, to suffer, to bring. Words bear nature's wisdom. Bear's cognates are birth, bairn, bier, bore (tidal), burly and burden. Old Norse has *bara* ("a wave, a billow"). Celtic has *inverness* for *estuary*, "a carrying in." Bear's Latin cognates give suffer, offer and fertile. The Greek stem bears amphora, metaphor (born across) and euphoria. The image in *bear* seems to be hands and wombs: wise old midwife, storm-wracked pippin creaky with fruit. Words endure, birth and bring nature's wisdom.

NATURE:
The intrinsic qualities of a person or thing; "He was good natured." *Nature* is the order and essence of the physical universe, the "Laws of Nature." It is the outdoors, enjoying nature, reality, "the nature of things"; and lastly the processes and functions of the body, "the call of nature," coming and going. All these senses resonate in the phrase *Words Bear Nature's Wisdom*. Inner and outer, our souls and the wilderness meet in this word, nature. Words bear our nature's wisdom. Words bear her nature's wisdom. Words bear its nature's wisdom.

But nature is not abstract, not imprisoned in the world of our notions. She, we, and it live in places, contexts. (A context is something woven together.) Nature is expressed differently all over the earth. The tree in truth may be an alder or cedar here, a redwood in Marin or an oak in England. There are a myriad of trees representing a myriad of ecosystems. What tree grows in your heart? Without a place, without some special soil, our words lose resonance; our images thin without a specific reference. Without a place words become hothouse plants grown in our heads. We become tourists riding jargon buses, viewing nature from air-conditioned comfort. Language needs a place to grow. It wants humus, compost of image and experience, rings of weather. Words are the clappers in the weather-driven bell of the world.

Nature is rooted in Indo-European gene: a root woven into so much of our speech. *Gene* gives us ("gene, kind, gentle, genius, kingly, innate, gonads, germinate, gingerly, kindle, and nation"). *Natio* is the goddess of birth. Nature echoes in all these words. She is a multivisioned being, gentle generous genius in and about us. Careful speech brings us closer to her; words bear her essential wisdom.

> WISDOM:
> ‘Wisdom has two roots vis from Indo-European *weid* (“to see truly; I have seen, I know”). From this root we have vision, wit, wizard, evidence, Veda, witness, idea and history. The root notion in all these words is “seeing is believing.”

Dom is a suffix denoting state or condition. From its root we have Old English *dom* (“law or decree”). *Dom* is also kin to Middle English *deman* (“to judge, condemn, to doom”). (Wisdom is the verdict of sight.) Lastly *dam* is kin to *doom*. (Wisdom is the doom of seeing.) Words bear the doom in nature’s vision. Words are nature’s verdict, her *sentence*.

Commons and Community

Tonight I've been invited to talk to aquatic and marine educators about community and commons. But I would miss entirely the spirit of community and commons if I didn't acknowledge that the heart of what you're about to hear was quickened, tempered over 25 years of conversation with my beloved wife Sara Mall and that whatever insights blossom here are born of our communion.

A couple of years ago, Sara Mall and I traveled to Western Ireland in search of salmon folklore. The rivers around Dingle still have viable salmon runs. In fact, there is a lively little creek that runs through Dingle. Strolling by the creek one day, we noticed three old men seated on a stone bench puffing pipes and gossiping in Gaelic. I thought if anyone can tell us about the salmon, it's these old 'geezers.' So I stepped up and asked the first one, "Are there any salmon in this stream, sir?" He lowered his pipe and announced firmly, "No salmon here!" "Maybe he's daft with age," I thought and asked the graybeard next to him. "No salmon here!" he replied with some irritation. Still, I could not believe my ears and turned to the third smoky sage who hissed, "No salmon!" before I could open my mouth. Still, something didn't make sense and we walked down to the docks in hope of finding a fisherman. We found one mending his gear on a tidy double-ended boat. I asked him about salmon in the creek and he echoed his fuming elders, "No salmon here!" In desperation I asked, "Do you ever catch salmon around here?" "Oh, yes," he replied, "next month the place will be full of salmon!"

It struck us with telling force that these men were part of a community in touch with the commons. Salmon were an occasion, not an idea or symbol and, more, they were a shared occasion. Community and the commons meet truly in the present tense. What those old men were saying was that it was not time for the salmon and the seeming abstract nature of my question was almost meaningless. To them, salmon were the tongue that rang the bell of home, a silvery resonance that had its time and place, a note felt and enjoyed by all.

I began salmon restoration work as an idealist. I thought the work would bring me closer to home, the natural world surrounding us. I have lived here 30 years and that sense of occasion, the storied synchrony between human community and the natural commons, has just begun to dawn on me; salmon are no longer an idea, they are a felt presence—the landscape is haunted by salmon. And as I have learned and rehearsed salmon's keystone role in Northwest ecosystem dynamics, that haunting has blossomed into a vision wherein salmon are sea-bright silver shuttles weaving our rain-green world. From marine carbon in riparian flora to winter wren's occasional pecking the eyes of a spawned-out chum, salmon are the ties that bind. Consequently, I have come to imagine that we are all threads in a mystery—water shrew, elk, slug, sinner, saint—all expressions, words the Earth is speaking, intoning a language we are just beginning to learn, and salmon are the secret grammar of that vernacular, the language the Earth speaks here.

Words are important to me. Language is every bit as ecologic as nature. We are its weather. Language has a history, and is constantly evolving; words become extinct, migrate and change their habits and habitat. Tonight I'll pause occasionally to look more closely at a word, the way you might stoop to examine an oddly shaped mollusk, or focus your microscope into deeper magnitude. Words belong to families. Words born of a single ancestor, a root word, are called cognate, which means "born together." *Community* and *commons* are cognate as are *commune*, *commonwealth* and *communicate*. These words all sprout from a single root. The oldest, deepest root is Indo-European *moinis*, which means ("gift or exchange"). The Latin branch of that root is *munus* ("a gift or civic obligation, duty"). *Munus* gives us *munificent*, "wealth making, generous." It also sprouts *remunerate*, to "pay back." When you couple *munus* with *co*, you *co-munus* ("obligatory gifting together, mutual obligation and promise"). This root sense of mutual obligation and promise is what informs community, commons, communicate, even immunity, which originally meant free from obligation, free from civic duties.

Seen from the root word perspective, the commons is nature's shared and interrelated gifts and the obligations they imply. Human community is a shared sense of gift and obligation. The natural commons is the larger community that contains and sustains human community. Traditionally, the customs and culture of human community are synchronous with and gratefully respectful of the larger context of the commons.

In traditional culture, we eat salmon and our bones eventually feed the trees that shade and feed the waters that give salmon life.

Unfortunately, we no longer live in direct contact with the commons. Our civilization has become a mechanical contraption that cruises through the commons imagining it can short-circuit the traditional obligations to the commons with cyber stretch technologies like genetic engineering. But despite our clever techno-wizardry, we cannot escape the fateful truth that human community, its vitality and survival, are grounded in the munificence of the commons. For most modern people, daily experience is removed or buffered by convenience technology from the grave and radiant poetry of the commons: alder leaves drifting down to blanket salmon carcasses, red-legged frogs hopping solitarily through the forest brush bound for a pond they cannot see but know its exact location.

No, we no longer live in and with the commons community. We live in an uncommon fantasy, consciously separate from the larger natural surround. We count ourselves privileged to be free from nature's thrall, its mortal beauty. And yet there is something missing in the prophylactic techno castle we feel so free in. What is missing is mystery. So we love to visit the commons where it abounds. But we come as tourists, not inhabitants, our feelings born in sentiment, not necessity. We find refreshment in the wonder of diversity—the co-evolved formal beauty of the myriad creatures of the commons, their mutual obligations and promises. But we don't belong to it, no longer depend on it directly, intimately. We are co-evolving with computers, not salmon. McLuhan was ominously correct—the medium is the message.

The commons is nearly synonymous with ecology. Ecology comes from two Greek words: *Oikos* ("household, dwelling place"), and *logos* ("narrative, speech, talking, storytelling"). So ecology is the story of the dwelling place, the house tale. Curiously economics has a similar etymology. *Oikos* ("house-hold, dwelling place"), plus *nomos* ("distributor"). So economics is household management. *Economos* originally meant ("steward"). The two words are sympathetic where the steward tends an economy based in the commons.

But our house is no longer the commons; rather, it is a system of self-rehearsed machinations called commerce, an institution that has little sense of home. Western civilization has abandoned the security of being part of the story for the dubious comfort of a profit and loss statement. We now belong everywhere and nowhere.

But for most of our history, we belonged to places, the way salmon belong to streams. That is why the world has so many cultures and languages that grew contained and contexted on islands, behind mountains, separated by rivers and seas. We co-evolved in all the eco-tones of the planet and the wealth of human cultures and languages, witnesses of thousands of years of intimacy with Earth's diversity.

Our psyches, arts and languages were nurtured in the mutual obligation and promise of indigenous realms. Our language witnesses the places where we achieved our humanity. Indo-European peoples evolved their cultures in forests; we know this because our word truth traces its roots to an ancient word for tree. *Deru*. This root gives us trust, truth, truce, tryst, betrothal and tree.

The truth is like a tree: leaves catch the light, the bark protects the sap wood that circulates vitality, the dead heart wood holds the tree up in the wind, the leaves take in the light, the roots mine the ancient earth-born nutrients of the ancestors. The truth is like a tree. No wonder we troth, truce, trust and tryst in its shade.

The commons community is still grounded in places; weathers, geologies and water regimes conspire (or is it commune) to shape plant and animal commu-nities into special ecotones over millennia. Ecotones that become dynamically complex and subtly nuanced in the local communion of community. Summer chum salmon have been returning to Chimacum Creek for at least 8,000 years. Indigenous peoples were just as loyal to places. But times have changed and people of the industrial age follow career paths, not the seasons, and in our dubious and privileged mobility, the commons have become a place to visit, not to work. Resources once dignified with sacred respect are now commoditized materials we see in board feet and pounds of oysters. Our relations with the commons resources are mediated by machines, not prayer. Resource comes from Latin *re-surgere* ("to resurge"). But digging deeper, we find surge has another root—*sub-regere* ("ruled from below"). So a resource surges back, ruled by powers hidden from view.

Our civilization has become a kind of Earth satellite, kept in orbit by the resource gravity of the commons. Yet the more we consume, the weaker the gravity of the commons becomes; someday the commons will let go of us. (*Consume*—destroy utterly by fire; hence *consumer*—neighbor, comes from a root that means near fellow-dweller.)

So in a kind of pre-industrial nostalgia, we come down to Earth to play, but not to live. Our obligations to the larger community of the commons are sublimated into corruptible, arbitrary laws rather than the co-evolved customs of accommodation and exchange. I learned last night that our state department supervising eel grass beds has ruled that an invasive species of eel grass, an annual rather than the native perennial, has been okayed as a remedial substitute in destroyed or disrupted eel grass beds. I wonder what the herring and salmon smelt who co-evolved with the perennial form of eel grass would say about that if they could.

We all sense the precarious health of the commons that support us and know that somehow we have to re-integrate our communities into the life of the commons, re-establish community, communication and communion with the commons. We have to re-synchronize our lives and livelihoods with the commons if we are to survive long term. But how? It won't happen by fiat or government regulation. Money can't buy connection. It will happen if we have a change of heart.

Your heart will one day say "don't move, stay put." The longer you stay put, the longer you are located, the deeper your experience of the local commons and the more you encourage your neighbors to form their community in and around the commons. You fly-fish for cutthroat at the mouth of Chimacum Creek, count coho redds in Fauntleroy Creek in Seattle, play poker with third-generation loggers and fishers in the back room of a Shelton tavern, or read poetry in a rain-drummed crummy with tree planters on a logging road up the Dosewallips.

The first obligation of the new community of the commons is to stop moving. Communities whose populations turn over every 15 years are not liable to be loyal or curious towards the commons that sustain them. Salmon are dedicated to a locale, fir and cedar are dedicated, calypso orchids are dedicated, we alone consume the munificence of the commons without accepting the customary co-munus, the mutual obligation and promise everyone else abides by.

I realize staying home is an idealistic and difficult promise for us freedom-loving, mobile moderns to make. It will take a long time and persistent will to exchange our wheels for roots, to become neighbors rather than consumers. But it is not impossible!

I believe the people in this room are playing a pivotal role in evolving commons-based communities in places they love. You are aquatic and marine educators. Education comes from a Latin word *educere* ("to lead out, bring forth, rear"). You are a special combination of guide, midwife and parent, which sounds about right for the marine educators I've met. The public needs to be educated and encouraged into becoming part of the commons, to re-enter the house rather than speculating on its value.

You are part of the lucky few in this age whose livelihoods are intimate with the commons. Yours is a new intimacy; traditionally, humankind was intimate with the commons as hunters, foragers and harvesters of the commonwealth. Traditional people had common sense, a sense of shared community. They lived within their means, took enough to live in gratitude, and encouraged the larger community to thrive. Along the West Coast from Santa Cruz to Yakutat and down the East Coast of the Pacific from Siberia to Hokkaido, indigenous peoples practice many versions of the first-salmon ceremony, where the first salmon was ritually cooked and eaten by all and where sometimes the grease was rubbed on the bellies of children. Its bones were usually returned to its natal waters in the belief its spirit would tell the other salmon people to bring their gifts to local people.

Your life and livelihood in the commons is different—you spy on the commons, watching and witnessing, returning to us with news and revelations of its wonders. You lead us back to open our eyes. You are the shock troops of reconnection, the Sacajawea of re-entry to the most real work, the commons. You are trained in the methods of science to focus on the object of study, but your work is to educate, to lead the public into a deeper awareness of the commons community, to leave them curiously inspired on the doorstep of ecology. And while your science is necessarily impeccable, I'll wager that privately the creatures you inventory, survey and witness the life cycles of are not objects or even objective to you. I'll bet you love them, and because you know how they live, love and die, they have become more *thou* than *It*, perhaps even "people" in the sense indigenous people used to describe the creatures of their community: salmon people, raven people, otter people. You witness a community of *thou*(s) but, true to the scientific discipline of your profession, only share these perceptions and feelings informally with close friends and colleagues. You teach the public eco-logic and save the ecolegends for your friends and children.

Science is a powerful tool. By excluding the subjective perspective, it assembles an understanding that can be tested, shared and believed. Science is self-critical and self-regulatory, deepening and expanding knowledge, mapping the unimaginable complexities that compose our world. Science documents the community of the commons, the structure, chemistry and tempo of mutuality. *Mutual*, by the way, is an etymological first cousin to *community*. Science builds windows for that intimate witness where the smolt transform into youngsters, but it does not instruct us how to feel about such wonders. Feelings are relative and unreliable to the scientific perspective and, hence, science shuns subjectivity because subjective imagination invites confusion. The data get sticky.

I am an artist. Our discipline is to trust the subjective because its honest loneliness invites inspiration as well as confusion; it's worth the risk. But science is right to be suspicious of unfettered subjectivity. Left alone in a boundaryless self-referenced perspective where every thing is relative, subjective creativity becomes absurd, produces art with minimum apparent meaning and long footnotes. But imaginative witness in context (*context* means "woven together" as in ecotone novels or communities), subjective imagination contained by a real place is self-sorting and self-organizing. The containment of context encourages the imagination to depict relations, articulate a world that is related, not relative. In context, the imagination's witness is tempered and tuned by generations until the commons is represented and understood as a story. The eminent Rumi scholar Colman Banks once remarked something to the effect that "story is as essential to culture as facts are to science."

The stories quickened by the subjective imagination in context and told over and over in that same context come to embody the truth of the tree rather than the truth of fact. But the truth of the imagination, disciplined in context, and the truth of science are not oppositional, but resonant. Native Americans lived with salmon for thousands of years and evolved stories that are uncannily sympathetic with the latest findings of ecology. Local cultural ethos is explicit, science's ethos is implicit. The difference between native culture and science-based civilization is that native people lived in the light of their understanding while we quibble in the shadows over the legal and proprietary implications of our knowledge. The necessity for the human community to reconnect with the commons is crucial, and you are leading the public towards that connection.

The stakes are high and time is short. The public needs to be informed but, even more, the public needs to be inspired. I think it is time to meld objective science with a dash of subjective art, to encourage art and science to tryst occasionally behind the tree of truth. I don't mean researchers should do watercolors or write poems. But I can imagine you educating the public from another perspective—a viewpoint that encourages and quickens the restorying of the commons, because it is through stories that it will truly be resolved. Community completed by communion.

How could it happen? I imagine a marine educator explaining the ecology of eel grass scientifically, laying out the food webs, the nutriment cycles, the crucial role these play in salmon and herring life histories and the complexities of life forms dependent on eel grass, and offering a metaphoric story that begins, "It's like." A story that condenses and personifies the dynamic of the eel grass community into a narrative explicit and memorable—an artful, articulate rendition that inspires listeners and makes them part of the story. A story that reminds the listener that we are members of the commons, even if we pretend we are not.

Or a marine educator could conspire with a writer or artist, meet behind the tree, and commune, communicate until they find the story, each perspective an aspect of the subtle "joinery."

Another example: Jeff Cedarholm has been documenting salmon-based nutrient transport and salmon-based food webs in Northwest ecosystems for years. His work needs the transformative energy of a marine educator—a poetic conspiracy to condense his work into an artful story that can charm our collective heart back into salmon sanity.

It is through the artful articulation of the commons that we rediscover communion. The commons and its creatures begin to re-inform our vernacular, our language relocates in locales, finds its metaphoric strength and depth in the resource world, not the ephemeral homeless cleverness of technology.

The resonance between human community and the commons won't happen overnight. It will take stubborn retelling and refitting the stories by generations of people willing to stay put for the transformation to occur. But remember we are in the inevitable tow of ecologic gravity, not economic haste. Ecosystems spiral slowly forward in time, evolving, and if they are to survive, economies will have to eventually synchronize with the ecologic tempo.

My hope is that artists and scientists can cooperate to change the focus of human endeavor from wanton commerce to careful community. (*Focus* is the Latin word for *hearth*, "the place where the local gods dwell." Ainu people passed all game meat into the house through a window directly in front of the fire so the resource, the power hidden behind the veil of flames, could see they were treating its creatures well.)

Community and commons naturally coalesce into culture. We don't enjoy real culture. We consume fragments of culture decor floating in a torrent of distraction and entertainment. We pretend to the boredom and ennui of royalty with our demands for continuous novelty. True culture is place born. *Culture* comes from the Latin verb *colere* ("to till the soil, to walk around a place"). Its past participle is *cultus*, hence ("culture"). *Wheel* is a close relative of *culture*. Culture turns with the seasons, it is a mobius striptease revealing and concealing in its turning. The soil is the past, the ancestors—all that went before, salmon, trees, parents. We turn the soil into the light so it may bloom. Each day is a marriage between the past and future. What we call ourselves, human, comes from Latin *humus*—our name means soil born.

In ancient Ireland there was a belief in a creature called the salmon of wisdom. This mythical creature was said to live in the well of Buan, the great nature goddess. The well was surrounded by magical hazel trees whose fruit fell into the well and fed the salmon who lived there. Sometimes a "pretender," an innocent future king of Ireland, would chance upon the well and the all-powerful Buan. If he could survive her riddled invitations and win her heart, they consecrated his kingship by making love by the well. The well echoed their passion and overflowed into the five rivers of Ireland and the salmon escaped to return to bless the unexpected with wisdom.

In one village an old wise woman once dreamed that a man of her village named Finn would catch one of the salmon and by tasting of its flesh would become the enlightened avatar/king of Ireland. Of course, every family named their first son Finn, but after some generations and no luck with the wise salmon, the practice subsided and Finn became just another name.

Well, there was one lad who believed he would catch the salmon of wisdom and set to fishing on the grassy banks of the Boyne (Buan's river). He became an adept fisher and eked out a living supplying the village with trout and salmon. Finn, in his old age, knew all there was to know about catching fish and one rosy evening when he saw a dark swirl near the far shore, knew it was a large salmon and cast expertly just ahead of its eddying wake. His knowledge paid off, for when the salmon broke water to shake the fly, there was the salmon of wisdom, scarred, draped in torn nets, pierced by broken spears, adorned with all manner of hooks.

But Finn was old and weak and the salmon, huge and powerful, began to pull him down the grassy bank into the river. In desperation, old Finn cried out, "Help me, help lest this great fish drown me!" And who should be walking along the river that evening but young Finn headed home after a day playing hooky from school.

So young Finn ran down and helped old Finn pull in the great fish. Exhausted, the old Finn said, "Young friend, thank you and if you'll be so kind as to cook this salmon and give me the first bite, you can have the rest to take home to your family." Now young Finn was from a poor household and knew this fish would bring him great credit in his parent's eyes. So young Finn built a spit, cleaned the fish and began to cook it. But as the fire was a little too hot, the great fish began to blister and young Finn, in absentminded care that the fish not look poorly cooked, reached out with his thumb to pop the blistered skin. Well, the fish was hot and greasy and young Finn's thumb was sorely burned and he thrust it in his mouth to cool it.

Sucking his fish-greasy thumb, young Finn could suddenly understand the language of birds, could hear the song the grass was singing to the rising breeze and knew why the old Finn wanted the first bite; this was the salmon of wisdom that the village wags joked about.

So young Finn confessed his mistake to the elder Finn, who graciously allowed that he had become wise enough in his 65 years by the Boyne and that it was fated that a young, powerful man should become Ireland's savior. And so the young Finn became a great hero. But whenever he was faced with a great decision or intractable problem, he had to suck his thumb to see through to the truth.

Smart, Not Wise

Eighty-two years ago a warrior from the Mount Lassen region of Northern California stumbled, starving and half-mad with grief, into Oroville, Calif. The sheriff found him huddled by a slaughterhouse corral fence, surrounded by barking dogs and curious townspeople. The genocide against his people had ended 30 years earlier. But the last survivors of his tribe—the warrior, his mother, uncle and young niece—had survived as watershed ghosts. They swept their tracks, cooked on smokeless fires and ate only salmon, small game, roots and plants.

Despite their considerable skill at secrecy, they were discovered by a power company survey crew. Fleeing in honest fright, the uncle and niece perished fording a flood-swollen stream. The warrior carried his invalid mother to a secret place and cared for her until her death a month later. For the next three years the warrior lived a grief-stricken nightmare, bereft of family, terrified of the whites closing in around him. Finally, in a kind of suicide, he burned off his hair in a traditional show of mourning and stumbled into Oroville to meet his fate. Luckily, the sheriff contacted University of California (UC) anthropologist A.L. Kroeber, and the Yahi warrior was taken into his care.

Kroeber, more than any other person in California, knew who this man was—a traditional Native American traumatized but unvanquished, untouched and unchanged by industrial society. Kroeber knew a few Yahi words and won the warrior's confidence through his respectful treatment. When Kroeber asked the warrior's name, the refugee answered simply, Ishi. *Ishi* was the Yahi word for "man" and being a traditional person, Ishi could not reveal his true name. He was known as Ishi until he died.

Ishi went with Kroeber to the UC Berkeley museum in San Francisco and worked as a caretaker and anthropological informant until his death in 1916. Before Ishi's death, Kroeber asked him his opinion of modern society and its "conveniences." "Smart, but not wise," was Ishi's laconic answer.

—

Reflecting on Ishi's perception of our "way," I discovered that much of our daily speech reflects his perceptive distinction between wisdom and smarts. For instance, we now say "bottom line" instead of fundamental or basic, thereby shifting the metaphoric heft of the concept of essential grounding from foundation to commercial credit. The origin of this spoken value has been transferred from the good earth to a ledger.

Although we seem fatefully inclined to smartness rather than the wisdom Ishi embodied, our language is grounded in a tradition of wisdom similar to Ishi's and etymologies (origins of words) offer the same practiced witness. Many word roots (etymons) reflect an older, more balanced relationship between humans and nature.

For thousands of years, humankind perceived the natural world as part of the family, worthy of care and respect. Nature was a thou, not an it. The hyper-rationalism of the eighteenth century and Newton's now obsolete but nevertheless brilliant reduction of nature to mechanics "dehumanized" the natural world and made possible the Industrial Revolution. Nature de-souled, explained in reductive mechanical terms, allowed its denigration into property and encouraged its abuse. The "mechanization" of nature allowed us to wantonly exploit the natural world. Our understanding and relationship to our home places changed from a neighborhood of generational responsibility to one of proprietary power over speculative assets, "property," real estate. It's a fine line between alienation and abstraction. We abandoned our homes to make a "killing."

—

The rise of extractive, reductive capitalism and its obsession with property and profit embody the opposite of Ishi's imagination wherein the world is an assembly of *thous* not an inventory of *things*.

It is only in the last 200 to 300 years that we have become so obsessed with property, profit and power. For most of human history, despite the profligacy of elites, culture was closer to Ishi's wisdom and the roots of our words reflect this.

Consider our word *material*. It sprouts from the Latin root *mater*, which meant ("tree trunk") as well as ("mother"). Cut down mater and you produce *materia*, Latin for ("lumber") or, put more directly, ("mother-substance"). *Mater*, the mother tree, is still haunting us; she is the dark echo of our materialism.

Ishi's distinction is also evident in the words we use to express "verity." Presently, we discriminate only slightly between fact and truth. Truth has more natural weight than fact, though we'd be hard pressed to explain why. A look at these words' roots confirms our intuition. The basic sense of fact is something done. The root is Latin *facere* ("to make"), hence ("factory, fact, feat, fashion"). There is an ambivalence in fact's sense of itself. How was the fact produced? A fact isn't really firm until we know its history, its agent or author. Some facts have multiple agents and authors. It is only the shuttering of our curiosity that allows us to polish facts into data and input. Is a bee a hive being, a future queen, or a device of a flower to fertilize itself? The "bee fact" is simply the radiant nexus of all those stories.

What about truth? Truth grows from the Indo-European root *deru* or *dru*. Deru meant tree; its progeny are ("tree, truth, durable"). *Druid* (*dru* plus *vid* "the one who sees the tree, trust, truce and betrothal"). In the imagination of our ancestors the truth was like a tree and so it is! The truth and trees are alive. A tree "eats" light and transmutes its mystery through the alchemy of chlorophyll into carbon and water. It stores the mysterious food in its roots. In fall, a tree sheds its leaves to the ground where an infinity of organisms compost (compose) them into soil, humus. (*Humus* is the root for ("human, humility and humble").

—

The tree (durable truth?) cycles all this energy, informing it. Roots feed leaves in spring and leaves breathe in light and the carbon dioxide waste of other creatures to feed the roots and breathe out the air that inspires us all. The roots pull minerals, dissolute stones, old bones, the bodies of all that dies nearby to grow the tree (truth?). The heart of the tree is silent, resinous and dry. The tallest tree is supported by its still heart; only its skin, leaves and roots are truly alive. In these ways, a tree (truth?) stores and restores its place. The life of a tree vitalizes the metaphoric heart of truth; irreducible, it defies our attempts to cut it up and cook it into data, without succumbing. You amble around the truth; you don't have the truth, you meet it; like Buddha you dream in its shade.

Words and their roots reveal older patterns of relationship. Etymology is really an exquisitely condensed folklore that precisely witnesses the character of our experience. Wisdom is stored in the roots, and dictionaries are full of deep dreams. But moderns ignore roots. War and depressions have taught us that money makes a slippery world. We slide away on it, homeless.

Ishi admired the cleverness of our machines but saw through them. He liked locomotives because they were huge, dreamlike and scary and he was a warrior. But he didn't like shoes. He said they broke his contact with the earth and hurt his feet.

Curiously, *smart* comes from an Old English word meaning to feel pain, sharp pain, hence able to pierce, hence smart, hence shrewd, clever. In contrast, *wise* buds from the Indo-European root *widein* ("to see"). One sees, one knows. This root yields ("evidence, witness, wisdom, provide and wizard"). *Smart* and *wise* represent attitudes. Smart is sharp. Wisdom is remembered witness. Wisdom is the care for a true story; smart is dividing the spoils.

Tradition tells us the smart should serve the wise. Rather than dividing the spoils we can begin to witness the truth here, smell the cedar and the fir, and re-enter the assembly of Thous.

Stump

There is a fir stump near our old well by the creek. I cut it for firewood fifteen years ago. It isn't large, maybe eight inches in diameter, and was growing in the shade of a larger fir until I cut it. I didn't pay much attention to it after I turned its trunk to wood. Then years later I passed it carrying water to the barn and I noticed it was healed over, like the stump of an arm missing its hand, a concentric cumulus of cracked bark, a scar armoring the end of its empty reach.

Fir trees don't usually heal over, so I made a point of showing it to the local Department of Natural Resources forester. He explained that the mycorrhizal roots of trees intertwine and actually communicate chemically, and that the larger tree (still green and standing) probably sensed the wound to the smaller tree and "instructed" it chemically and nutritionally to heal. Which it did. It now appears as a handless arm that's lost its grip on the light, or has it? It shows no sign of rot; it's still rolling bark over the old cut, still alive in the shade of its mentor whose own green hands continue to catch and share the day.

Homecoming

In the early nineties our local salmon restoration group undertook a stock restoration project to rebuild the summer chum runs on two east Olympic Peninsula streams, Salmon and Chimacum creeks. In September, fisheries agents trap chum spawners in a weir and take a percentage of the eggs. These eggs are "eyed up" at the Hurd Creek Hatchery in nearby Sequim and then turned over to us to incubate in a small hatchery we built on a tributary of Salmon Creek. By protecting the eggs, we can boost the egg-to-fry survival by almost 100 percent and hopefully build up the run. We watch the eggs until they hatch, and then feed the fry to a certain size and release them to their sojourn in the sea. Seven volunteers alternate checking eggs and fry daily from November to late April. We are committed to this project for at least ten years. We hope to rebuild the Salmon Creek stock first, and then transfer Salmon Creek fish to the chum-barren Chimacum system.

One clear January day I was at our little homemade hatchery checking water temperature and flow, alert for the early hatch that sometimes occurs in a warm winter. I lifted the lid on the incubation barrel to check on the 46,000 eggs, the progeny of twenty wild chum hens, supported by black-screened trays, vibrating and rolling delicately in the smooth rhythmic shade of the water flow. It is always a little eerie peering into this watery womb, and I leaned down to study the eggs' opalescent glow. I was trying to decipher what the subtle changes in egg color meant; I was wondering at the dark sentient density of their eyes. These eggs can see, and that day I had the uncanny sensation that two eggs in particular were watching me. They followed my motions, rolling and twisting to "see" me—it was unnerving. As I closed the incubator lid and began to write up the daily report, I had the eerie intuition that those eggs were the eyes of the watershed, venerable and rejuvenant in the same moment. It was as if 8,000 years of watershed experience, the biologic, the patient wisdom of Salmon Creek, was coiled in those two vigilant eggs.

Driving home, my hatchery encounter brought to mind a Fraser River Salish story I'd read years before. In the story, Swanset was married to a woman who was one of the Sockeye Salmon people. Newlywed Swanset lived in his wife's village and ate with them. Each evening his mother-in-law would come up from the river carrying a salmon in her arms like a child. She cleaned and cooked it in a respectful way and called Swanset and her daughter to eat. Swanset's wife carefully washed her hands before eating and cautioned Swanset to do likewise. The old matron warned him not to break the salmon bones but to lay them carefully to one side. At meal's end, the mother-in-law gathered up all the bones and returned them to the river. Each evening upon returning the bones and ambling up from the river, stately in the twilight, she was followed by a young boy who rollicked in circles around her. The Sockeye People were glad to see the merry lad; he was a vivid witness and a celebration of the rightness of their way. Swanset was curious about the miraculous child, and so one evening he kept one of the salmon bones hidden in his mouth. When the boy appeared that evening he was lame, unable to dance and leap. Angry and suspicious, the villagers confronted Swanset. His father-in-law, the chief, threw him to the ground, retrieved the bone and healed the crippled youngster, who joined them by the fire.

The genius of Native wisdom is to return the bones—complete the circle and honor the gift by giving back. It is this spirit that blossoms so beautifully in the image of the boy frolicking around the dignified grandmother. Our genius, the industrial trick, is to crack the circle, mine its wealth and move on. In our contemporary story the boy doesn't dance but preens sulkily in the rearview mirror of a car, radio blaring, while the grandmother is singing down by the river. The boy is afraid to leave the mirror's enchantment and celebrate her miracle.

Maybe it's as simple as this. In a consumer society, sustenance is a spare transaction: we buy fuel to hurry into the future. For traditional people, food is sacramental and eating is often an act of remembrance and hope. We can't go back to the past and we can't follow our present course into the future. We need a new-old way of looking. Musing on the profound difference between our quick-witted consumer culture and the sustained wisdom of traditional neighborhood cultures stirs a childhood reminiscence worth retelling.

When I was a child I loved marbles. I had a big wooden box full of cat's-eyes, aggies, "puries," clay marbles from Mexico, stone marbles from North Carolina. When spring came and the ground had dried, recess would find us racing across the schoolyard to an old oak tree in whose shade we would draw our circle on the cool, clay ground and play.

We laid out our risk marbles, picked our shooters and lagged to see who would shoot first. Every marble had a meaning and each of our marble bags held an anarchist chess set. The marbles had histories and personalities. Some were heroic, some beautiful, some old and chipped. But all possessed a kind of marble soul. You rolled these marbles around in your hand like a strange seed, a fossil bone or arrowhead.

We played ferociously and hilariously. The best player was a raven-haired girl named Marcia who hooted and leaped, talking to her marbles like fish in a stream or make-believe grandchildren far from home and in danger. It was a mythic drama we enacted in those dappled green days, a kind of fateful dreaming that required all the qualities adults were coaxing in and out of us in their formal way—daring, skill, practice, strategy and imagination.

But there was a minority of players who didn't see it as poetically. These players would inevitably propose allowing "steelies" into the game. Steelies are polished-steel ball bearings from three-eighths to three-quarters of an inch in diameter. Steelies were a technic fix. They required only good aim and a strong thumb, and whoever went first with a steelie usually won. Other marbles couldn't budge them, and the risk marbles and shooters that were our imaginary friends became fodder in a bottom-line game—win at all costs. Every year we voted steelies out; our game was a theater, a magical circle, not a get-rich-quick scheme. Ever since then the phrase "losing your marbles" as a metaphor for insanity has had a special resonance for me. I think it is the same deep seriousness of that childhood initiation into the natural heart of culture that inspired thoughtful communities from Japan to Northern California to take responsibility for their local salmon runs. The circle in the clay resounds with the cycle broken, and further with our forsaken spiral into the bottom-line solipsism of steelies.

Governments and most businesses play with steelies. They must—we hold them accountable to standards of efficiency, not to beauty or soul. They probably won't save the salmon, because they are distracted by the perennial cacophony of special interests and the pursuit of profit. It is the locals, the neighborhood people, with small circles and vernacular marbles, that may be the truest and most useful constituency for the salmon. What better agents than ourselves to revive our region's salmon runs? We are the natural kith to their kin. We marvel at the miracle of their return, argue over their health, and rise early to troll and mooch for them in the dark testy weather of the North Pacific. We ceremoniously savor their firm yet delicate flesh, subtly cooked in a myriad of local and family recipes. In smokes, spices, sauces and glazes the salmon is the soul food of the North Pacific. And while they delight our senses the salmon also represent us in a profound and heartfelt way; they are the precious mettle of our watersheds, they embody our home places. Salmon are the deep note of our dwelling here, the silver soul of this green bell—steelhead, sockeye, coho, chum, pinks and kings.

But be warned against restoration romance. Salmon restoration is a paradox more salted with irony than leavened with heroics. Because we assume responsibility does not mean we're in control or will succeed. The salmon know what they're doing. The mind of the "leaper" is tuned to geologic time, and our entropic, superheated civilization may be a minor perturbation in their world. I can imagine salmon of the twentieth millennium spawning in the moonlit rubble of the Kingdome. Perhaps the question for salmon is how big will civilization grow before it consumes itself? For us the question is, can we get back in synch with the salmon cycle in time to bank our fires in a suitable hearth. Restoration work is really reinhabitation; community building with all the "neighbors."

If you try to restore salmon to your watershed you soon discover the neighborhood is haunted by salmon. The gravel road I drive daily was built decades ago in the middle of a stream. It was the easiest way. Once a small salmon-rich brook, it now trickles schizophrenic in ditches on either side of the road. The brook's cycle, the flow, pulse, quality and quantity of this watersheds' water has been drastically altered not only by misplaced roads, but by conversions of forest to pasture and dwellings, short-rotation timber harvest and impoundment of this once-spirited rill in ponds that make fish passage impossible. Even if the cutthroat, steelhead and coho that once homed to this unnamed stream could follow its scent home, they could not navigate the tattered threads of its unraveled waters. Following the salmon home is labyrinthian daunting work.

Revisiting the history of the salmon's decline in our neighborhoods is depressing, but stream work and habitat revival is full of high-spirited comradeship and the small epiphanies of recognition and connection that bloom when what you've done actually works. I recall the chance witness of a coho parr leaping into a culvert we laddered for fish passage two summers ago. I remember the glee with which we greeted one small fry in a rill that we reconnected to its main stream, and also a couple of cutthroat fingerlings nestled in the scour pool behind one of the boulders we'd placed in a stream that was down-cutting because it had lost structure (wood and stone) and couldn't dissipate its energy. Discrete, vivid moments like these weave us into place. They reconnect us to the complexity and wonder of the natural world, rekindle our imaginations, and edge us away from the unconscious thrall of consumption and back into the quickened drama of creation and community. Restoration then becomes restorying the landscape with tales of its essential beauty.

Imagine a Thanksgiving dinner of your great grandchildren a hundred years from now. In the center of the table is a bright silver salmon locally caught and cooked in the practiced way of long enjoyment and reverence. At the end of the feast there will be a simple ceremony—a long walk to the creek with neighboring families, each with a wooden bowl of salmon bones, to return the remains to the waters of their creation in gratitude and respect. Perhaps there will be mention of the ancestors, if that is who we decide to be—the old ones who stayed put, who gave the salmon shelter in their hearts and who found their own way home.

Fish Tickling

Fish tickling is a kind of secret surprise, the capture of wary prey under water by means of a subtle invisible caress, a subliminal seduction wherein the prey wakes up suddenly in another world. Fish tickling is an ancient skill—no tools, nets, hooks, weirs or spears, just your own hands and intuition quickened in a deft concordance of silent sensitivity.

My friend Les Perhacs can tickle fish. I saw him do it once. We were drifting down the Duckabush River in wetsuits and snorkel masks while the summer chum skirted by in their funereal calico wedding regalia. Les was the leader of our little band of novitiates, pilgrims, variously astonished witnesses of the river's radiant clarity and its mysteriously clued crosscurrents of yellow, green alder leaves and the bruised ardor of the chum salmon.

We stopped to rest at a pool edged with great ice-rounded boulders and fringed with sword fern, alder and cedar. The rest of us sat silently reflecting on what we had seen. Les crossed the pool and was standing with his back to us facing the rock- and fern-ledged bank. He began to edge slowly up and down in the currents below the overhanging bank. He moved the way a carpenter moves to check the plumbness of a wall or a dowser moves over a vein of water, a sort of slow-motion, short slip-stepped jig trying to line up something subtle but intensely real. He kept his hands below the water and beneath the bank searching the river shade. Back and forth, slowly up and down the bank he danced; then he stopped dead still except for a slight lingering motion of his elbows. It was as if he were playing an underwater piano or were a blind man weighing precious rare eggs to determine their fertility. All the while Les did not look down; his head tilted back just slightly, all his attention focused in the dark liquid shadows around his hands. It looked like he was trying to remember something. Then he stopped entirely, stark still, expectant and keen as a seedling turning to the light. Now he held his arms tight against his waist the way you might hold them to carry a sleeping child and turned in a slow motion arc to face us. He was beaming with glee as he slowly lifted his hands out of the river to reveal a sleek, sun-dappled steelhead who for a moment was as still as our witness, then woke to our world's burning air and flipped shaking into the leaf-scaled rill of last year's rain and was gone. Les's laughter leavened and confirmed our amazement.

Years later I asked him how he did it. He said as a boy he learned to hypnotize birds by gently running his finger from the crown of their heads to the end of their beaks. Later, night diving off the coasts of California and Mexico, he taught himself to steal into the dark world of rock-laired fish, miming the water's feathery flux with his fingers, barely brushing their throats and bellies, slowly coaxing confidence in his water-rippled touch, muting their instincts with subtle insistence till they accepted the dreamy cradle of his hands and let him lift them where he would.

Imagine if we were on the other side of the tickle. What river are we in? What is tickling us, thimbleberry blossoms in the nether-world? What strange air will we awake in? Life is rife with surprise.

Home/Hag/Wife/Clue/ Focus/Surprise

Our word *home* blossoms from the Indo-European root *kei* ("to lie down, to be recumbent"). This root nourishes the words civic, city, hamlet, cemetery and Shiva, among others. In Old English it appears as *ham* ("home, a house with land"). *Ham* has a derivative *hametan* ("to house"), which is related to Old Norse *heimta* ("to bring cattle home from pasture"), whence the Old French word *hanter* ("to dwell in, to frequent"). *Hanter* becomes English ("to haunt"). Home is a place wherein we rest, dream, and return. Home is the familiar haunt, the grave dwelling of concordant dreams.

Hag derives from old Germanic words for hedge or woods. A hag is the woman on the other side of the Hawthorne hedge, a woman of the woods, a wild woman, untamed.

The word *wife* is the green edge of an ancient word, *weip* or *weib* ("to tremble, to vibrate"). *Weip/weib* also animates ("wave, viper, whip, waiver"). In Old English *wif* meant ("woman, married woman"). In most archaic Germanic languages wif meant woman primarily and "wife" secondarily. Semantically the old Germanic words for woman (*wif, wib, weib, vif*) mean either "the vibrator" or "the veiled one." The veil vibrates in her world's mysterious wind; is she signaling or inviting?

Clue or *clew*—from Old English *cleowe, cleowen, cliwen, ball, skein*. These words are akin to claw, cloud, cleat, clod, and, perhaps, clown (originally a country bumpkin, a clodhopper). A ball of thread in ancient Greek myth and fact was used for finding one's way out of a labyrinth; hence a means of discovery, hence a discovery that assists in the solution of a crime or mystery. A clue is the end of an unraveled ball of thread, the beginning of an unraveled whole. We walk and wind, gathering our way into the light.

My friends used to laugh at my old Latin teacher, Mrs. Gleeson, a hunchbacked crone who clacked her false teeth in furious punctuation when she read aloud from Caesar's *Gallic Wars*. But I secretly loved her because she revealed that words have souls or at least roots, and are alive as you and I. She taught us that if you honor the heart of a word, your imagination feels a deeper gravity, a richer calling.

We learned that *focus*, a word with Etruscan roots, before its current meanings of clarity, intensity and effciency, originally meant hearth. Focus was the dwelling place for two families of deities, the Lares, local gods of landscape and nature and the Penates, gods of the house and home. These deities of the inside and outside world were embodied in the hearth fire, *focused* in the flicker of our mortal witness. We worshipped them in the baked mud house of the hearth. So originally, *focus* was not a synonym for *precision*, but a name for the local prescient mystery resurrected daily by a simple spark and our spirited breath.

The hearth is the heart of a household. Households are confirmed in marriage. Marriage is a shared and consecrated hearth, husband and wife focused together, kindling a common fire, sharing warmth, chopping wood, cooking and bathing, attending the perennial surprise of children, tempering their vivid heat into focus, honoring the local gods inside and out.

Every morning husband and wife blow the dark, dream-dim coals of wonder back alive, back in focus.

Each day we sweep up the hearth's ghostly ashes for the garden, lay the day's fire and listen to the ancient gods of our common life whisper from the flames dancing in witness before us now.

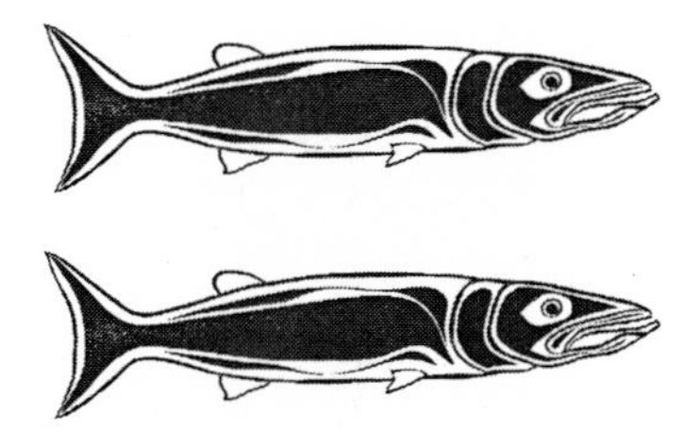

SALMON WOMAN & RAVEN

The photographs on the following pages were taken at Tom Jay's casting studio by the late Mary Randlett and offered to the author as a gift. They illustrate the process of casting the sculpture entitled "Salmon Woman & Raven." The captions were written by the photographer. The bronze sculpture is large at 16' x 16' x 16'. It was a public commission for the City of Bellevue, Washington, in 1991. Today it stands in Highland Park, in Bellevue—Ed.

The artist constructs the original from
which molds will be made.

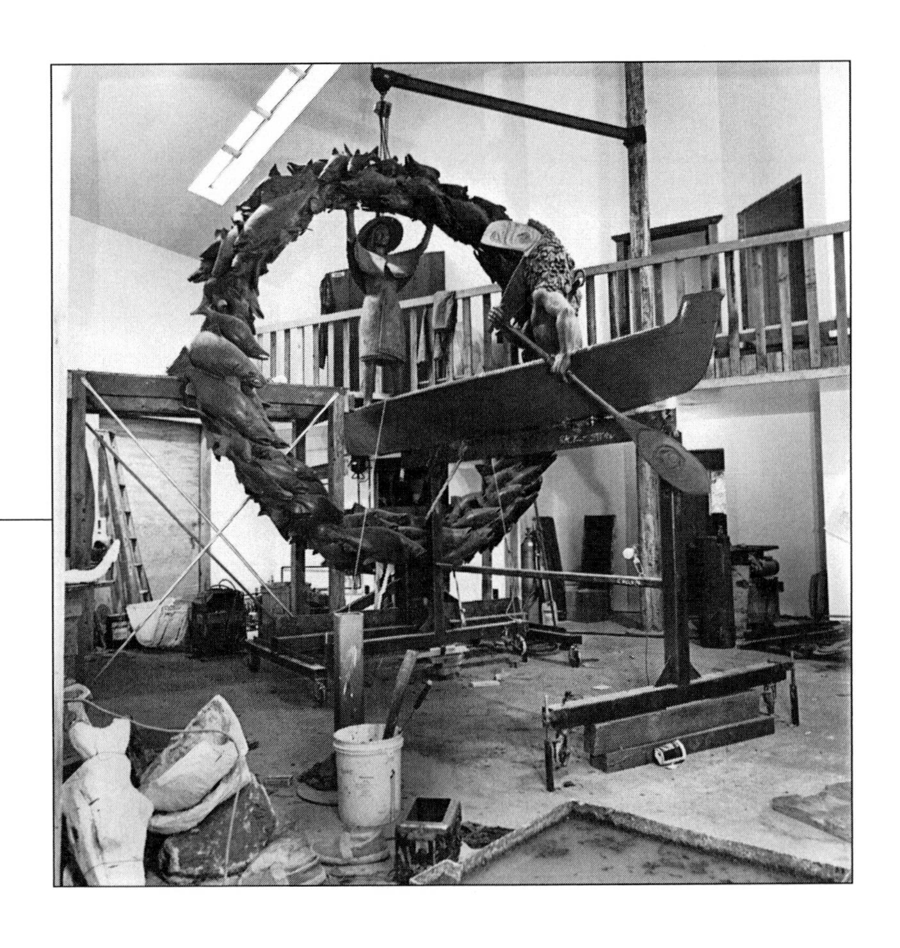

The rubber mold is applied to
the salmon ring.

Wax is applied to the rubber mold to
establish thickness of the metal.

Mold is removed from the
salmon ring section.

Waxes are removed from the mold and the sprues applied (sprues are the waxes which will form the channels through which molten metal flows into the mold).

Investing sprued wax in plaster and sand mix to completely enclose all wax systems.

Fully invested waxes go into the burn-out kiln to melt out all wax.

Pouring 2100° F bronze into a section of the salmon ring investment.

Investment is chipped off
the hardened casting.

Cast metal emerges as more investment is removed.

After the sprues have been
cut off, the last of the investment is
sandblasted off the casting.

Chasing (finishing) the bronze castings.

Cut

Welding the finished castings
into salmon ring.

The metal casting
fully assembled.

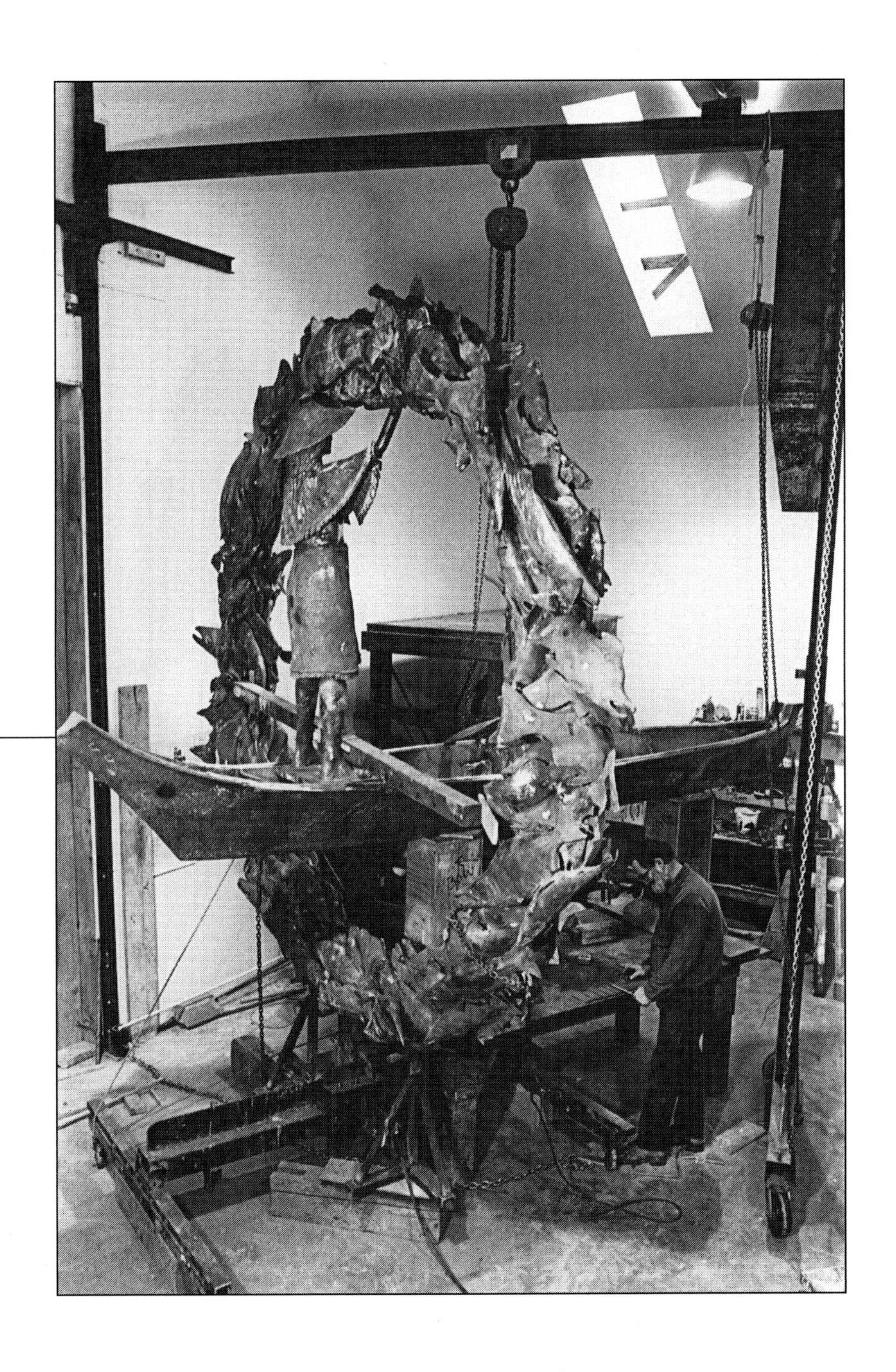

Applying patina chemicals to heated metal to color the finished sculpture.

Installing the finished sculpture.

The finished bronze sculpture.
Salmon Women & Raven.

Crossing Hood Canal Bridge

It was clear.
A cat's eye day.
An old farmer friend and I
had just dropped the winter's pigs off to the butcher.
On the way home we talked,
he pointed to the land around us and said:
        "When I first came here, it was terrible.
        The loggers had been everywhere, ruined
        trees, nothing held the ground water, wells
        went dry. You could buy land for fifty cents
        an acre. Ruined. Where I came from
        trees are rare, still the greenness
        of this place brought me back."
and I thought:
        "They learned late, the farmers,
        the loggers, the highway builders.
        Men who gloried in their youthful
        strength and saw too late the ruined
        forest, the barren ground, the preposterous
        roads. It is a bitter old age for
        them, tuneless and grim. They know
        they ruined the bell they rang
        so fiercely."
And yet:
        A few men always know. My friend told of a harvest
        time long ago on the high plains,
        when his father, seeing another man
        mistreat his own horse,
        whipped the miscreant to his knees
        with a dead black snake.

A Slip of Silver

A luminous dream cradled in the muffed
rattle of creek-worried stones, an eyelit shadow
coiled in the fertile mercy of my egg...soon I will
swim up sleek into the sun dappled wake of water
and flash, a slip of silver in the braided babble
of my sea-mad stream.

Who are we?

My salt-wise soul, grown nimble and dark
with blood in the treacherous feed of the sea, gyres
the ocean's pilgrim-haunted swell and in the third summer
of its winding catches,
like an orphan startled by
his mother's eyes, the scent of the grave-strong
stones of home and dashes in water-shattered
moonlight back into the rainy wealth of his nativity.
Hook-nosed, bruised, gravid tatter-finned dragon of the
brook, my canny strength gone into milt or eggs, spent
like a dying man's last tithe, I cast my life back to the
endless roil of stones and drift away, a dazed
feast for a tumult of hunger, my ruined beauty
borne on in every body, deepening the inevitable
soil and its fateful dream of trees.

Who are we?

Throne Poem

Time is a hive
of incredible bees;
working the world;
enjoying and nurturing
its star-fed strength.
We are, each one,
the hive's own queen.

Speckled Dream

I went to the sea
for myself.
She fed me health,
new legs,
perhaps a speckled dream
to wrestle in the night.

Pond

Still water seems to see.
Note the pond's alder-lashed eye
unblinking,
even in the ice-blind
gray of winter.

Faithful pupil focuses the wind-stirred,
star-haunted crucible of sky
remembers each winding season
in its dream-dark, water-sifted reverie.
The long patient wait of water
presses the weather-ciphered pages of its text:
blossom, pollen, seed and bone,
blossom, pollen, seed and bone.

Hunter's Song

Striking,
stricken.
An eagle with a fish too big to lift,
I answer from my place.

Stones

Stones,
time's hard skulls,
blind mutes,
polished frozen loaves of fire.
Stones,
mountains down on their luck,
mystic dice
slow rolling
in the earth's incredible dream.

Landscape

House-sized rocks
moved hundreds of miles
by rivers of ice....

Fire-tempered trees
nursed skyward
by the bones of ocean-blessed fish...

A thousand songs
wait unquickened
in the rain and wind.

Storm

All night the storm
cracked and hissed in the treetops.
The old green gods
throw off their dark disguises
and dance in the fierce fault of night and day,
until the silent morning sun calls them home
behind their masks of cloud, wood and stone.
Only the broken fir limbs
and the scattered cone purses
recall their wanton revels.

Plainsong

Everyone is alone.
Fledglings left in the nest,
we even learn this alone.
Solitary we turn from dreaming
to the empty air around us...
in
to the plain girl in your heart
who is finally asked to dance.
She doesn't know that
you are death.
You would be kind;
dance well.

Klamath

Starless twilight
chicory blossom sky
crone's blind eye
focusing into darkness.

West wind haunts
the river valley
dry and leathery
as an aged Yurok widow's breasts.

Who is it
rustling live oak and madrone
with a fierce woman's touch
coaxing the summer fruit to earth?

We row hard
into this ancient prescient wind
on rafts pieced from parts
of a thousand nameless places
glad to have come this far together.

Masquer

Masquer,
you hide in me
like a snow owl
            in the wind.

Coasting in my own
            unsteady breeze
you hunt hidden and alone.

The Well

I dug my well in fall;
down through till and sand,
down in time
in blue till and clay
hunting a vein
ants and willows whispered over
all summer long.

I had my trusted tools,
strong simple magic,
an old truck axle
forged to break stone
and a rusted shovel
with a twice-busted handle.

A spade and a wand,
I held half a gypsy's hand
and I worried it with work
while I waited for the draw.

I chose a shape,
a path to follow down.
A circle this time,
last winter I dug
a square dry hole.
A circle for luck
and I dig it twisting into the earth
Coriolus even here...
The well spiraled down
miming the motion of its prey.

Down into the ground,
busting my body
in her hard gray flesh—

strange love of men
deep in the earth,
potent in mines,
in wells.

I worked on,
earth louse
hunting the blood
clouds buried there.
Last year's rain
crawled beneath me
in the stones,
cold thin wisdom whispering below me.

A slow spinning dancer,
mole patient,
I sank in the graveled dream
by the labor of my hands.
Down in time,
stepping through the fire
asleep in stone,
through red sparks
and the slow sulfured breath
of broken minerals.

Hunting a vein
I found treasures
buried eons.
Blind old stones
brought to light,
round crystalled rooms
opened accidentally;
and one day twenty feet down
a fist of black smoke
trapped in a ball of sand.

At night I dream of fountains,
baroque fantasies,
burbling angels of copper and lead;
and a black lake
buried ten thousand years
rising hungrily to greet
my forewarned feet.

I think of this well as a tattoo
on my grandmother's breast.
Think of it as a place
to store the songs of a drunken friend.
A well is as simple as this:
plain hard work,
you tap the earth;
break it open
and lift the pieces out.
Working down in earnest
you try to wake the water up.

Walking to the Barn

Walking to the barn
in the cold blue twilight
of this wintry day;
the water bucket steaming
to make warm mash for our toothless horse.
The horse is older;
the bucket heavier with the passing years.
We duck beneath the breeze-supple branches
of a young cedar seeking the
open light of the trail.
Its green brushes us as we pass,
Mall stops and whispers,
"To be touched by a tree is a blessing."

Beauty

Beauty is the world's gift
passed on in honest witness.

Cleverness may catch it
but stills its soul in clutching.

We stand on the edge
of a grave that wants a garden,
waiting for heart's old drum
to find a song.

There is no art
          for art's sake.

The blossoms are ghosts
          at the wedding

Eve

The red fruit refreshed Eve.
But the apple smoked in Adam's hand
like a coal.
And it was not her fine free care
he felt that day,
but some vague bearded fear
that made the sky go dry and cold;
a fear that poisoned clouds
and made Eve's smile grow old.

Elders

Salmon slap the work-scarred,
earth-curved decks of fish boats
like blind abandoned angels knocking
at a midnight door bereft...
The starry quicksilver glint of the sea
suffocating in our mortal air
and then
I've heard them slash the laughing rills
on moonless winter nights
dodging clawed phantoms
in the rock-creased stream.

But today watching
a water-bright bruise of dog salmon
brawl over this haunted gravel
for the first time in a decade...
I close my eyes and dream of
silver-skinned elders,
the old ones, spent and
weeping in welcome
for the clear-eyed rain.

Arrival

A moon-white moth
flutters easy as a magician's hand
in the candle-lit air...
searches the house
like the inside of his hat,
then disappears
just as you arrive.

Dru Oja Jay
born 2-3-80

Remains

We grow thin in time; our shadows stick.
The world presses our practiced skin
closer to our bones.
They wobble tree-slow almost stately
in our bodies' sea-soaked breeze.

Our well of tears surprises us;
we cry quietly at the funny parts of movies,
circus foolish in the approaching confusion.
No longer heroes we become
bewildered hobos in the screaming iron
boxcars of our remembering.

The tempered armor of our learning,
rusted stiff and thin
by our own strong weather,
is useless now. So we step out and
catch the fateful train
over the snow-white mountains of winter,
our tatter-veiled nakedness
the final witness
to the death-edged innocence
that remains.

Restoration

(for the Salmon Creek Crew—Cheri, Bob, Clif,
Bruce, Noreen, Robbie)

When the ripened life of summer coils,
quickened like a press of darkling ghosts
in the ruddy luminosity of these eggs,
we begin to nurse their intent.

Bravely, as if we know their secret,
we attend these tender beings,
who are loyal only to the earth-sifted rain
and its sun-woven rivers.

Through flood, silt, disease
and the hungry shadows
of our pestilent civilization,
we have been faithful,
flirting on the edge of our common despair
with wonder.

Love

(for Sara Mall)

Love is not a flower.
A rose is the afterthought
          of love...
with its fragrance,
its thorns
and slowly fading colors

No, love is a root.
The water-split seed
drives deep into the ancient earth
to find strength to seek the day.
You are my drop of water
you are my darkest treasure
you are the honest sky.

Winter Greeting

The machine won.
Its clawed mind
caught us all,
enthralled.

Yet somewhere
in the pale dawn dark
of the snow-still forest
a woodcutter cradles
a frozen axe blade in his hands,
warming its bitter edge
against the daily work.

Sifting

A true secret
is passed secretly

like night rain
falling between the terrible stars,

and if not secretly
then humbly,

the fire-folded loaf of stone
waiting unbroken in the road.

And if not humbly
then honestly,

a blind man dancing
to heart's old dream

And if not honestly
then kept,

secret

a dark bird
silent in the royal dusk.

Loki

Fire,
the licking secret hidden in wood,
makes our amulet words,
molding its laughter in our two-eyed echoes.
Doubt it?

What is it then that edges us and all we see?
Not dreams nor time,
but some grim flickering force
a bright imperfect hunger.

Lasting Light

The bright poets
strike their tempered steel
against the flinty world,
sparking a brief sacrificial radiance
that blesses life's tumult in its fall.

The shadow poets
sing another way;
at home in the abiding silence,
they feed the haunted hearth
their weathered wood.
Blowing on the storied coals,
they coax forth a smoky
longer, lasting light.

Drunk Song

This road is gray cotton
for my eye's slow wound.

This car is full of
bees and babies.

My heart is a poisoned arrow
fired aimless in the night.

Names

> *"Star thistle, Jim Hill Mustard,*
> *White tops, Chinese lettuce,*
> *Pepper grass, the names of*
> *Things bring them closer."*
> —Robert Sund, *Bunch Grass*

Names are ghosts
that lead us home, home to old houses
full of working spiders
and webs taut in shadow and light.

Names are winds;
small breaths
that open doors and close them.

They are honed lenses
breaking light
that otherwise would blind.
They are tools to make time.

Names are fate's osmotic flesh,
living cells robbing meaning from the sun
and dying in their time.
Names are a lame man's curse on dancing.
They are weird skins dropped on moving mysteries.
They are flayed seals barking
in a circus far from the sea.

Names are gypsies knocking
at your back door selling charms
and hexing your home if you do not buy.

They are odd winks,
incisions, wounds

and weddings;
they are the two-timing sweethearts
of our souls.

Post-modern

When the garden
is blooming mechanical flowers
the parents become scarecrows

Bangor

When it comes
it will be quick.
Your old high school sweetheart
will be making tuna sandwiches
for her kids
in a stucco house in Poulsbo.

Young Ed from work
will be getting his hair styled
at the mod barber's in Bremerton,
hating the thought of swing shift,
envying the old men playing pool
across the street.

That strange girl from days past,
you could never figure her out,
but it hurt when your buddies
mocked her strangeness.
She will be scuba diving in Hood Canal,
looking,
just looking.
Your oldest boy
will be reading the P.I. on the ferry,
home for the weekend,
thinking about quitting school again,
troubled by problems
neither of you see.

When it comes
it will be quick.

The heat will peel
your old sweetheart like a grape.
Light blinded

she searches bravely
for her moaning children.

Ed is cut in half
by plate glass,
an infinity of surprise
in the barber's mirrors.

And that girl
you could never figure out,
that strange girl,
Barbara,
will be carried by a wave
into the tree tops
speared by a burning fir.

Another wave will catch your boy.
The red hot ferry will hiss
as the wave wraps its cold fist around it.

Where will we be
when it comes?
It will be quick.

We are coaxing it home,
wooing it down into the strike zone;
the perfect pitch,
the last out,
inevitable.

Stirring a bad dream with easy lies
we will awake in flames.

Ghost

In daylight
a ghost is a winter tree,
leafless in the slanting storm;
it's green gone underground
dreaming with wren bones
and the echoes of summer's lost songs.
This wraith is not dead...
there is no death.
The simple gravity of spring
tows its pale sun-gyred hunger
back to life,
up into the day to catch its light,
to coil seed and cast it,
to haunt doom's dark wealth
with bloom.

But in the deceptive rest
of night's oceanic silence,
a ghost is the iridescence
of light's long fall refracted
in the mortal waters of our moment;
its broken radiance redressed in colors
so we know it's real.

People

Waiting for the Seattle ferry
in the exhaust and impatience
and two crows drop
like black tattered books from the gray
unlettered sky, fold the ragged
pages of their wings and strut,
bluffng each other
for a piece of stale bagel.
"Crow people," I mutter,
surprised at their humanity.

Science

Science is the plain view of wonder;
the unrelenting record of a world
whose secret compass is your heart.

Science is not life but life's echo scripted,
the constantly revised notation of a symphony
impossible to perform or conduct.

Science is logic's spy in the burning palace of awe.
It is the well spoken secretarial ghost of the real.
Churched in reason's dry witness;
it is the unblinking keen of worldly love.

Return

Fear, booze, the rat-faced brawls,
the bluffng wit and broken promises...
the bitter sweet wounds of women
turned to salt...

Born to water
but afraid to swim
I polished the spook-toothed sea
into a circus slippery mirror.

Each morning I comb
my unruly vanities into style.
The actor's waxy ruse masquerades as meaning
and the mask fattens in the clownish smile
of intrigue and false imagination.

In my murky mirror
love is a stillborn secret
drowned in the leaden paint of my lies.
Finally the mirror fails its fatal fascination and falls,

shattering into a desert of splintered light.

Beware this is not death;
but death's refracted keen,
her note.
Rooted naked in her stark call
I may still climb the apple-breasted trees of time
and list at last the laughing birds of innocence.

I will let her patient gravity
sift myself as simple soil
and invite the dark to whisper;

to invite my soul to dream
that the ghost green, seed-cracking shoot
of my life may wave above earth's grave wisdom

tapping at the empty sky to rain.

Snow

We waited for the snow
the way children wait for sleep.

It came falling in the darkness—
ringing the air in mystery,
a thousand moths in a black stone bell.

It was the final snow of winter,
and we danced in it like wounded birds
          and laughed.

It was a snow of revelation.
It was the cloak of a ghost
wrapped close enough to see.

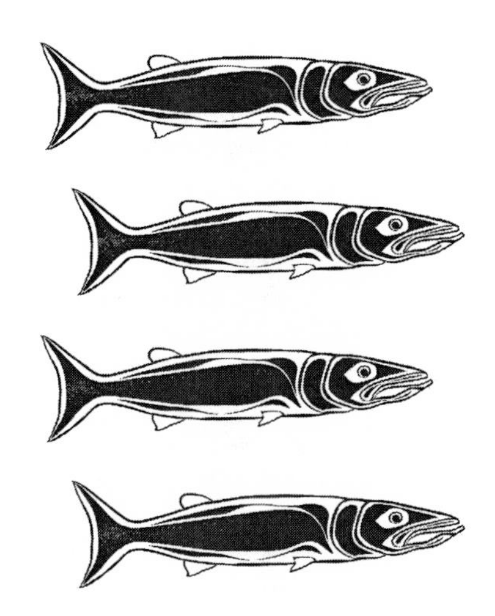

Little Gray Brother

In my youth I was an All-American boy. I got good grades and participated in student government and the debate society. I loved contact sports, football and boxing. In fact, my identity was framed by these sports until my sophomore year in high school. My doctors discovered, after an especially hard hit in a football game, that I had a congenital weakness in my lower spine and a risk of permanent paralysis in my legs if I continued playing.

There I was, a young man without a mask. When I got to college and discovered booze, my aggressive impulses darkened into self-destruction. Country-western taverns and biker bars tested my mettle. I spent more time drinking than I did thinking.

I ran with rebels of all sorts—jazz pianists, existentialists, you name it. Contact sports had metamorphosed into brawling with the tangle of the ineffable. One night after too many beers my jazz pianist friend and I decided to test God. We snuck into a local church and lit all the candles, waiting for God to strike us down. It was night and anyone could see our blasphemous bravado glowing in the church windows. Someone called the cops. My friend had a longer list of misdirection and misdemeanors. He was expelled from the college. I was given nine days in the county jail and probation with warning from the college.

The county jail was about thirty miles away; the college was east of LA where there were still remnant orange and avocado farms. Once a week a sheriff's bus would stop by the local jails of the little towns that speckled Highway 66—Ontario, Claremont, Pomona, Azuza and San Gabriel. At every stop new prisoners would get on the bus and get their ankles and wrists chained to a long chain that ran between the seats on either side of the bus.

We were a polyglot offspring of the historic migration that alloyed the vitality of California's working class; North Carolina folks who came west in the great depression and stayed to build the aircraft and battleships that helped win WWII. There were Mexican families who had lived in California for hundreds of years and were the true aristocrats of the place. There were Italians and Irish driven to California by political unrest and oppression.

As we drove into the city, we could see the smoke billowing up from the LA skyline. It seemed the city was on fire and it actually was. We were headed into the Watts riots of 1965.

Our bus was only one of many converging on the LA county jail courtyard. The city was burning around us. As we drove into the county courtyard, we were stopped to let the buses in front of us unload. There were at least ten buses with more crowding in behind them. As the doors of the buses were opened, police were waiting with billy clubs. The rioting passengers were not chained, so they had to be herded and beat into the jailhouse entry way. Everywhere on the buses were black men who were fighting back. It was an unfair, ferocious fight and the Watts men had no weapons. Dozens of buses unloaded hundreds of black men with more arriving all the time.

When our turn came, the guards told us to stand up and make an alternating line and walk off the bus slowly. At first, we complained that the enraged crowd of black men would turn on us. Then the cops with the clubs came on board and we obediently left the bus. All around us the unchained Watts men were still fighting as they were forced through the jailhouse door. Once we were inside the jail we were unchained and led to our cells. There was still mayhem all around us.

Mine was a six-person cell; two double bunks on opposing sides of the room and two more bunks at the end of the room. On the remaining wall was the toilet and sink. There were already four Watts prisoners in the cell, working men swept up in the riot. We nodded acknowledgment of our bad luck and didn't have much to share except our cigarettes. Listening to their occasional conversation I guessed they were skilled construction workers anxious to get back to work.

Around noon, there was a loud, violent commotion coming down the hall towards us, probably a prisoner from the ongoing revolution outside. They stopped in front of our cell, opened the clanging door and shoved the prisoner into our room. He was a large, powerfully built black man who had been clubbed many times judging from the lumps and split cuts on his face and head.

As the door clanged shut and the jailers moved down the hallway, he looked at me and said in a clear voice "What's this white motherfucker doing alive in here?"

He was staring at me. The room was suddenly dead silent. I had instinctively backed to the wall between the toilet and the sink.

It took a while for me to speak; I didn't have a clue as to what would happen next. Then I said, "I don't have a beef with you, we're all in here together."

The other four men were quiet, neither supporting nor denying the big man's curse on me. The wounded man said something like "You're not worth an ass kicking." I didn't answer and after a while everyone but him lit up cigarettes.

I was in the top bunk across the room where the wounded man was. I climbed in the bunk and tried to calm down, but I didn't sleep much. Imagine if the tables were turned and five white guys were in a jail with one black man. Remember the lynchings, shootings, castration and brutality visited on black people over the centuries? Imagine a decorated black soldier returning home to America as a veteran only to have his eyes gouged out by a sheriff's baton because he said the wrong thing. It's time to make amends, it's time to turn around.

The next morning the jailers came and put the clubbed man in shackles and took him away, maybe to trial. I don't know. But I do know I let out a deep sigh of relief as I climbed out of my bunk.

The older of the four men put his hand on my shoulder and said, "Little gray brother, you didn't have to worry. We wouldn't have let him kill you."

Ghost Train

I learned how to ride freight trains from my old college friend Rob Cooley, now sadly deceased. My introduction began when I asked Rob if he was going home for spring break. I asked him how he was going to get there. He didn't have a car, few of us did in those days. "I'm going to jump on a freight train, should be there in little more than two days."

"Are you kidding, isn't it dangerous?"

"Yeah, it's dangerous, but not if you're careful and know what you're doing. I'm going to catch a train two days from now; meet me at the Ontario train yard crossroads at one o'clock in the afternoon and I'll show you how I do it." I showed up a little early and walked around the yard. The screeching steel and hard thumps of coupling as the railroad cars were switched was a little scary, tons of wheeled steel making a train, coupling and uncoupling.

It wasn't long before Rob showed up. He had a rucksack on his shoulder and was wearing an old baseball cap for shade. "It can be hot in the southern California spring." Rob took me to a shady area next to what he figured was the main track west. His plan was to ride a westbound train to the main yard in Los Angeles and catch another train north to the Mackenzie River valley in Oregon where his family lived. Rob explained he had done this before—ride a feeder train west to the main yard and catch a train north.

He said we should wait half-hidden in the shade for the westbound train on the main track. I can't remember if there were whistles or some kind of signal when his train came into view. It was moving about ten miles an hour but slowly picking up speed. Rob waited until fifteen or so cars had passed. He turned to me and said this was the careful part, see you. Rob had picked out an empty gondola car and loped along next to the train until he hit his stride and was next to a ladder at the end of the gondola. Rob was a middle-distance runner in high school and college. He had that long, easy stride that allowed him to float up to the gondola ladder, grabbing a rung with his left hand and swinging up onto the ladder. He turned and waved bon voyage, climbed the ladder and dropped out of sight in the empty gondola.

I was hooked. Rob made it look beautiful, but I had to learn that I didn't and never would have Rob's easy stride. I'm a long-waisted Scotch Irishman, good for wrestling but not running down trains.

I either had to risk a fifteen-yard sprint or be sneaky and find cars I could hide in before the train left. Occasionally I chose the wrong train and wound up in danger or blessed with strange luck. The time I chose the wrong train I had ridden to Santa Barbara to see my ex-girlfriend. She didn't want to see me, so I was stranded. In frustration and ignorance, I chose a train that was headed to Bakersfield. I was hoping to catch a ride north to San Francisco but got confused and chose a train headed east over the worn-down Sierra mountains to the desert. In Bakersfield I walked up and down the trains looking for an open boxcar. There were many long trains, but all the doors were locked and there were no gondolas or flatbed cars. The only chance I had was a tank car with a steel catwalk. I hadn't slept very well before the Bakersfield yard. A tank car is dangerous but maybe the train would stop and switch in a few open box cars on the way.

The train chugged up into the hills east of Bakersfield. It was night and I was trying to stay warm and sleep on a catwalk with no railing. The train snaked along the ravines running up into the hills. I was thinking the tank car was dangerous and I was getting colder and afraid that I'd fall asleep and roll off the tank car down into the ravine. So I laid on my side stretched out on the catwalk gripping the welded struts that held it together.

I was so tired I began to hallucinate. I kept a tight grip on the struts and my eyes open so as not to fall asleep. Then the apparition appeared. It would float up out of the ravine and grab for my legs or shirt to pull me off the tank car. It had hollow skull-like eyes and a long, wispy shape. The apparition was a sort of luminous mycorrhizal ghastly mist, a disembodied hungry soul. On the last pass at my ankle the ghost got very close but missed and tumbled like clotted cat fur down into the ravine. It didn't return.

I don't really know what happened after that. I still have dreams in which I've jumped from the tank car onto a box car and grabbed the door mechanism with my fingertips and swung inside to the box car in safety and sleep.

Or I've dreamed the train pulled off on a sidetrack to leave some cars and pick up others and I found an empty box car and crawled in and gone to sleep. What I do know is that I woke up in an empty side-tracked box car. I was at one end and an old brown man was at the other end. The door of the box car was open. He asked me for a few cigarettes, and I gave them to him. I finally focused on the view outside the door. It was white and shimmery in the warm light of the desert morning. The old man didn't have much to say so I sat in the doorway and watched the cars off in the distance. I could see the bug-like shapes of the cars and trucks speeding this way and that on the other side of the flat valley.

It wasn't long before the clang-bang of the switch engine told us we'd be moving soon. I asked the old man where he was going. "West towards LA."

"Will we go through Ontario?" I asked.

"Yes." he said.

"Will you tell me when to jump when we get to Ontario?"

"Sure." And we smoked another cigarette in silence.

Soon we were out of the desert and into the remnants of the orange and avocado groves all around us, all the orchards being gradually destroyed by suburban blight.

It wasn't long before we were in the Highway 66 corridor; businesses, schools, manufacturing centers. About twenty minutes after entering suburbia the old man said to get ready to jump.

It was baffling how he knew where in the world he was. He was at the far end of the box car and could see only a sliver of the landscape. But he was my only guide, so I wasn't about to get smart about when and where to jump. A few minutes later the train slowed down to a fast walk.

"Jump!" he said and just that fast I was back in a place where I actually knew where I was.

The Whirlpool and the Ladybugs

A father and son had a chance to go on a whitewater river trip. The leader of the trip was an old college friend of the father. He said he would let them both come for free if the father rode the large, unwieldy baggage barge. The son had never been on a river trip but soon found a liking for paddling an inflatable kayak down the river with the rest of the crew.

After a day of paddling and confidence-building, the son wanted to leave the group and paddle ahead a ways. The leader described the lay of the river and the large rock that rose up in the middle of the river. On the right side of the rock were rapids that the son could easily paddle down. On the left side was a vortex whirlpool that he should avoid at all costs. Somehow the signals were crossed in the son's imagination and he paddled into the whirlpool. His kayak was immediately pulled from beneath him and he began a wild ride up and down, roundabout and down again in the laundromat from hell. All he had to hold on to was the kayak paddle, which he later said he held on to with a death grip...up and down, round and round until he finally caught a current that floated him out of the vortex and into the shore.

There still was no sign of the kayak. It wasn't long after that when the crew leader and baggage barge came ashore to find the son standing alone with the trusty paddle.

For the father the reunion was a revelation. The son had almost died alone in a whirlpool while he drifted down the right side of the river. All he could do was hug his son; words would not suffice. There was really no need to speak, only listen.

It was weird, his son said, "After I dried out a bit a cloud of ladybugs landed on me. It was as if they knew something I didn't know, one even bit me."

There was still no sign of the kayak. But when the group reached a bend in the river, a quarter mile from the whirlpool rock, it shot up into the air like a rocket and then shivered over onto its side and disappeared, not to be seen again as they rounded the bend.

Prologue to Ohode R.A.R.E. II Proposal

The alder, whose fat shadow nourisheth
each plant set near to him long flourishheth
—William Browne, 1630

Throughout the Coniferous Forest Biome the forested-watershed is the bio-economic matrix, linking farm, forest and fisheries. Here on the Olympic Peninsula, rivers spring from a central point and flow out in all directions, forming a radial pattern and shaping 4.5 million acres of land: a watershed mandala of extraordinary beauty and productivity.

Ohode was a group of people living on the Olympic Peninsula and working together in the realm of watershed politics. The name comes from the Makah, an indigenous people still inhabiting the Cape Flattery region and designates a multispecies community, "all of us." Tactics vary but the strategy remains: to protect ecosystems as the basis for the continuing evolution of this community; relating human social economic strategies to the Peninsula as a living whole.

Rare II is a Forest Service program aimed at reviewing all remaining roadless and undeveloped lands in the entire National Forest system. The Ohode proposal contains maps, photos, descriptions and evaluations for ten watershed segments in the eastern Olympics and was successful in obtaining interim protection for these lands [pending ultimate allocation]. The prologue reprinted below discusses the significance of roadless areas in terms of watershed values and was addressed to National Forest personnel.

We start with the rocks, the bones the life here hangs on. An early Eocene lava known as the Crescent formation is the bedrock of the eastern Olympic Peninsula bordering Hood Canal. In places the basalt is ten miles thick. All the watershed segments we are proposing for roadless designation occur on the Crescent formation.

The soil base (glacial till) laid down on the basalt is rather recent. The soils themselves were created by forest-ecosystems since the Vashon glaciation 15,000 years ago. Though it certainly varies, the basic soil profile in the planning area is relatively thin soils perched on bedrock. Needless to say, there is a high erosion potential throughout the area. Soil, one of the major components of the watershed-ecosystems in this region, is fragile and restless.

Bones, what of breath? The climate. Our moderately wet climate is created on the interface of mountains and myriad sounds and bays, fed and stirred by the Japanese current sliding by us slowly north.

Climate and geology, breath and bones, give rise to specific biological communities, flesh, ecosystems that reflect and refract the limitations of geology and climate. Ecosystems divide naturally along watershed lines. A watershed-ecosystem might be defined as a holistic system, the bones, breath and flesh of a specific drainage; a being, an entity, a living place (Margulis, 1975). A watershed-ecosystem is the living system that survives and sustains itself in a particular meeting of geology and climate. (Seawind and sunlight coax old bones to dance.) The biomass, the flesh of the watershed-ecosystem, enfolds the bones, "breathes" the climate; the whole of it is a balanced and balancing matrix. Because of the variability of geology and climate, one would expect subtle but significant differences between watershed-ecosystems. These differences would express the varying relationship of water, rock, and light. It is important to understand that watershed-ecosystems are self-regulating entities. In a real sense they are persons and the fact that other cultures have called them spirits and assigned them resident dieties is not inappropriate. Our "scientific" bias has us name them *systems* from a Greek word meaning *composite whole*. Whatever we call watersheds, our names acknowledge their specific, complex and in-formed natures.

Watershed-ecosystems have designed themselves through time by a process of trial and error (Curry, 1977; Vannote, 1977) to establish and maintain an equilibrium.

"With the retreat of glaciers came the first communities—the lichens, mosses and grasses—forming a living cover over raw glacial till; reducing soil erosion and evaporation; building up organic matter. Next, willow and cottonwood seedlings, prostrate on the nitrogen-impoverished soil. Then, the alders: hosts to the nitrogen-fixing bacteria. Nitrogen compounds leak from roots to soil. Leaves form a nitrogen-rich detritus. Organic matter accumulates. Community succession continues. As the alder thicket matures, hemlock and red cedar surge upward and shade out the alder. The new stands thicken. More organic matter is added to the soil. Conditions continue to change." (Planet Drum.)

The mature ecosystem balances between rock and weather, mediating and arresting the entropy of energy and matter. Coniferous forest ecosystems have evolved strategies for dealing with disturbances, periodic disordering pulses that unbalance the system (fire, wind, and minor geologic changes).

It is important to note that a watershed-ecosystem responds as a single entity to disbalance in any part of it. Everything in the watershed is "organic," co-involved. For instance, there is evidence that declines in salmon runs and falling fertility of some Idaho forests may be related. Salmon feeding trees, trees feeding salmon (Odum, 1971; Edmonds, 1974). The strategies a watershed-ecosystem invents to respond to disturbances are not accidental but are evolved over millenia. Evolutionary lessons are represented in the biomass. For example, recent studies point to fire as a major ecologic determinant in maintaining Douglas fir as an effective climax species in Western Washington (Martin, 1976). A whole successional pattern has been built around the ecosystem's expectation of periodic disturbance by fire! To regenerate areas unbalanced, made more entropic by fire, the ecosystem uses ceanothus, alder and other soil-building pioneers to prepare the way for more complicated, balanced systems that follow. These regeneration strategies could be seen as the instinctive response of an entity whose end goal is equilibrium and conservation of energy through biological systems where everything is used (Curry, 1977; Odum, 1971). (Sunlight transformed to matter and haggled over for thousands of years.) All this is by way of pointing to the amazing complexity and subtlety of a watershed-ecosystem. Aboriginal peoples were closer to the truth when they envisioned the watershed as a feminine deity, for indeed a watershed is a matrix, a mother, a system that nurtures the life within it.

The watershed is a finely evolved system, a matrix, a mother, if you will. How does humankind relate to the watershed matrix? Of course the answer is in infinitely variable ways. Still, we think it is informative to contrast two cultures' relations with the watershed-ecosystem.

Indian peoples indigenous to the Hood Canal watershed had a spiritual-physical relationship with the watershed. All members of the watershed community, from salmon to cedar, were acknowledged in a democracy of spirits.

Aboriginal peoples understood that they were but one animal among many; that people were part of, an aspect of, the watershed matrix. They were "organs" of the watershed matrix and all creatures in the watershed were literally of one flesh. There was a graceful confusion between humans and their environment that was refracted and clarified in their myths and stories. They had an extensive oral tradition that instructed them to their place and their organic role in the watershed matrix. They knew that to live sanely in the watershed they had to respect it, not control it. To them it was family, their body, the matrix of their living, a wise old woman's house.

By contrast, our model of the watershed is neither religious or scientific, as we often claim, but economic. Watershed-ecosystems are a resource to us, a soul-less source of raw materials. We envision, and hence treat, the forest rather like a biological mine (Silene, 1976; Krugman) where all we need to do is occasionally shore up the shafts and tunnels (replant and fertilize clearcuts) and keep on mining. We forget that frequent disturbances are something that the watershed-ecosystem is not prepared to respond to. Responses to man-made disturbances, such as short rotations of clearcuts, are not encoded in its genetic information. It takes ecosystems a long time to learn because they are so complex. If we continue to deal with the watershed in the crude mechanical terms of economics rather than as a subtle, holistic model, we may be wounding the watershed matrix without knowing it because our model won't let us see the wounds! We envision the forest in the crudest terms: dollars, soils, energy, and water. But our economic model excludes the subtle but crucial factors of non-game wildlife and non-economic plant species and their role in the health of the watershed matrix. While we may think we are "managing" the watershed well on the short term, our knowledge is woefully inadequate for long-term planning. We have little or no data of non-game wildlife, non-economic plants, and geologic information is often too general to inform site-specific planning. We really don't know how watersheds work in holistic terms. For instance, we know soil erosion rates before and after logging, but don't know the regeneration rate of soils (U.S.D.A., S.C.S., 1974). We lack critical information yet presume to set "acceptable" rates for erosion. This is incredible! Without knowledge of replenishment rates, current forest practices are like writing checks on an account with unknown reserves.

"It is, now, quite well demonstrated that site degradation occurs through nutrient and soil losses on any kinds of forest types, from southeastern Loblolly pines grown on old fields with a 60-year rotation to Douglas firing the Northwest. We need much more real research to determine rates of loss and replenishment of nutrients before we can accurately predict allowable rotation periods that will be possible under sustained yield" (Curry, 1976). We know that nutrient capital and soils are formed over long periods of time The watershed-ecosystem regenerates disturbed areas slowly through a succession of plant and animal communities. These communities build up nutrient capital and soils and are in turn succeeded by a climax ecosystem that maintains the accumulated capital in a fairly steady state (Fredericksen, 1972; Franklin, 1973; Edmunds, 1974). This takes time. Our economic time frame is faster, more lineal, than nature's holistic time frame. We're in a hurry to maximize timber production and profits; our haste forces us to abandon the ecosystem's proven regeneration strategy, replacing it with one that relies heavily on dwindling fossil fuel fertilizers and incredibly toxic sprays (U.S.D.A., 1977; Clark, 1976). It seems we can stress the watershed-matrix as long as we drug her with fertilizer and herbicides. What happens in 50 years when we're out of "drugs" and we've turned the forest ecosystem into a monocultural junkie? Since forest ecosystems thrive on genetic diversity, depend on it to provide appropriate strategies of response to changing conditions, we should strive to maintain genetic variety by letting natural systems manage themselves as much as possible. Following a strategy of monocultural, single-species forestry is putting all your eggs in a basket too easily affected by disease, insect infestation, and climatic changes. Worse, monocultures are only maintained by heavy inputs of energy. They are increasingly "uneconomic" because they require extra energy over and above that which the site supplies (Silene, 1976; Krugman). We have to stop envisioning forested watersheds as biological mines and re-enliven our science with aboriginal feeling, see the watershed-matrix as a generous "person," a mother perhaps. The older aboriginal model is truer and subtler than our economic vision. If models are lenses to look through and we want to see as clearly and deeply as we can into the nature of the watershed-matrix, then a merely economic model is simply not up to the task.

"The science of ecology provides us with a logic of integration: individuals join to form species-populations; populations join to form community-ecosystems; ecosystems join to form the biosphere. If we wish to integrate our cultures with nature we do so at the *level of the ecosystem*, which everywhere has a common structure and progression but everywhere varies specifically in composition and function according to time and place" (Planet Drum). We need to expand our model, make it inclusive of biological and hydrological values as well as economic values. Otherwise we run the risk of exhaustion of the watershed-matrix. To improve our model we need more information, generated by insightful questions that address the watershed as a whole. We should be asking, "What percentage of a watershed can you disturb and still maintain adequate levels of productivity and equilibrium?" or "Is it more 'economic' under a holistic accounting system, one that includes biological and hydrological values as well as dollar values, to let alder replenish nitrogen capital in cut areas before replanting?" (Terrant, 1971), or "How do different cutting methods influence flow and quality of water and the characteristics of aquatic communities?" or "What effect does fertilization have on nutrient content or fertility of water draining from treated forest land?" or "What happens to various pesticides when applied to land? How fast are they degraded? Where do they accumulate? And what effect do they have on non-target organisms and the ecosystems as a whole?" Before we decide how we're going to use our watersheds we have to discover what they are, how they work. If we do this crucial work, then such euphemisms as *sustained yield* and *fresh management* will have a truer ring. We should remember that biological systems are the most "economic" in the long run because they are the most energy efficient (Odum, 1971). If we intend to continue stressing watershed systems, then we have to find viable ways of repair and maintenance of watershed values which are biological and hence economically sound.

Lastly we would like to briefly address the issue of new roadless areas versus jobs. It has long been a timber industry war cry that addition of roadless areas to national forests meant fewer jobs. A report entitled *Oregon Economic Impact Assessment of Proposed Wilderness Legislation* (Kutay, 1977) suggests they are probably wrong. The report examines the relationship between costs of roading unroaded areas and investing the same monies in intensive management of already accessed high-fertility sites. The report finds that if capital slated for new road development were used intensively, managing already accessed sites, that it would yield more board feet per dollar invested. It should be noted that Kutay used *low* figures for road costs in his analysis ($52,500/mile), so intensive management may be even more profitable than he shows. Kutay also left out environmental costs, soil loss, regeneration failure incurred in roading and logging steep slopes with fragile soils. If we figure in those *real* costs, then the strategy of intensive management of already accessed sites is even more attractive. Kutay's figures on road costs ($50,000-$200,000/mile) are similar to Olympic National Forest road cost figures, so the report's findings may be appropriate to our situation. Regarding loss of jobs, the report suggests that intensive management practices would actually employ more workers per unit of timber output. The study traces the loss of forest-related jobs to private industry's mismanagement of resources (Gedney, 1975; Wolf, 1975; Beute, 1976), a foreign-trade policy that exports raw materials and imports finished wood products (Darr, 1975A, 1975B), increased capital intensive versus labor-intensive harvesting techniques, and, lastly, increased automation of lumber, pulp and plywood mills. Since 1950, for example, automation has reduced the employee/MBF ratio from 8 employees/MBF to 4.5 employees/MBF in 1970 (Kutay, 1977). A leading Northwest labor spokesperson summed up the roadless area versus jobs issue in these words: "When we're arguing over wilderness, we're actually just fighting over crumbs, and meanwhile someone is taking the whole damn cake." In short, Kutay's report shows there is no net economic benefit in terms of capital or job production through roading unroaded areas and that the real crisis in forest-related jobs is the result of industry's mismanagement of resources, a foreign-trade policy that betrays local labor, and heavy automation of logging and milling operations. The Oregon report concludes that there is a greater return on capital and more jobs created by intensively managing accessed areas that there would be if we were to open and log roadless areas.

Ohode believes it is time to re-envision forest management in terms of the watershed-matrix. It behooves us to inform ourselves about her "personality," how she lives and works. In this new vision, the long-term health of the watershed would be the final arbiter of any forest-management strategies. We envision evolving strategies that work through and with the watershed's own biologic systems. This might mean scaling down logging operations over the long term to accommodate labor-intensive harvest techniques that are less disruptive of the matrix. We envision longer rotations fitted to on-site characteristics, and encouraging cultural and economic uses of alder. We envision managing the forest in terms of non-declining yield calculated on a per-watershed basis. We would like to see management for nutrient budgets, sediment yields and watershed equilibrium. Under these conditions forest product diversity would match species diversity and our economics would be closely allied with the genetic integrity of the forest. We see including watershed maintenance, monitoring and repair (check erosion at source, restore natural processes to degree possible) as real costs that have to be accounted for in any realistic model of harvest economics. Above all this re-envisioning would require all management strategies to be appropriate to the specific watershed-matrix involved. The regeneration failure evident in the upper Dungeness area is a prime example of failure to match harvest techniques to site characteristics. In the case of the Dungeness, the harvest technique (clear cut) applied to this exposed site resulted in lethal soil temperatures that make regeneration impossible.

"We understand that successful reforestation is a series of interrelated steps, each like the links of a chain. Traditionally, the steps have been studied and applied almost independently. We need to evaluate combinations of alternatives, measure their interaction effects, and assess their relative impacts on timber management and other resource values. This will permit forest managers to select optimum combinations of silvicultural practices to maximize reforestation success" (Stewart, 1977).

If we can admit the personal, living nature of the watershed-matrix into our conceptual framework, actually acknowledge *who* the watershed is, we will find welcome in that wise old woman's house forever

LITERATURE CITED

Beuter John H. et al

1976 *Timber for Oregon's Tomorrow*. Forest Research Lab, Oregon State University, Corvallis, OR.

Clark, Wilson

1976 *Energy for Survival*. Anchor/Doubleday.

Curry, Robert R.

1973. *Geologic and Hydrologic Effects of Even-Aged Management on Productivity of Forest Soils, Particularly in the Douglas Fir Region*. Even-Age Management Symposium, Oregon State University, Corvallis, OR.

1976. *Update on Forest Management and Soil Deterioration*. Testimony to the House Agricultural Comm., March 24, 1976.

1977. *Watershed Form and Process: The Elegant Balance. Co-Evolution Quarterly*, Winter 1976-77, pp. 14-21.

Darr, David R.

1975 (a). *U.S. Forest Products Trade Policies: What Are the Options?* USDA Forest Service, PNW-41, Pacific NW Forest & Range, Portland, OR.

1975 (b). *Softwood Log Exports and the Value and Employment Issues*. Pacific NW Forest & Range Ex. Sta., PNW-200, Portland, OR.

Edmonds, R.I.

1974. *An Initial Synthesis of Results in the Coniferous Forest Biome*, 1970–73. *Bulletin No. 7, Coniferous Forest Biome*, US/IMP, University of Washington, Seattle.

Franklin, Jerry F.

1972. *Proceedings—Research on Coniferous Forest Ecosystems, A Symposium*. PNW Forest & Range Exp. Sta., USDA Forest Service, Portland, OR.

1973. *Natural Vegetation of Oregon and Washington*. USDA Forest Service, Gen. Tech. Report, PNW-8, Portland, OR.

Fredriksen, R.L.
1972. *Nutrient Budget of a Douglas-fir Forest on an Ex. Watershed in Western Oregon. Proceedings—Research on Coniferous Forest Ecosystems—A Symposium*. USDA. PNW Forest & Range Ex. Sta., Portland, OR.

Gedney, Oswald
1975. *Two Projections of Timber Supply in the Pacific Coast States*, USDA Forest Service, PNE-60, Portland, OR.

Gorsline, Jerry & House, Linn
1972. *Future Primitive, North Pacific Rim Alive, Planet Drum*, Planet Drum Foundation, San Francisco, CA.

Krugman, Stanley L.
Biosphere Reserves—Strategies for the Conservation and Management of Forest Gene Pool Resources. UNESCO US/MAB-8, Washington D.C.

Kutay, Kurt
1977. *Oregon Economic Impact Assessment of Proposed Wilderness Legislation*, Oregon Environmental Council, Portland, OR.

Margulis, L. & Lovelock, J.
1975. *The Atmosphere as Circulatory System of the Biosphere: The Gaia Hypothesis. Co-Evolution Quarterly*, Summer 1975, pp. 31-40.

Martin, Robert E.
1976. *Fire in the Pacific Northwest—Perspectives and Problems*. USDA Forest Service, PNW Forest & Range Exp. Stay., Portland, OR.

Odum, Eugene P.
1971. *Fundamentals of Ecology*, 3rd ed. W.B. Saunders Co.

Silen, Roy R.
1976. *The Care and Handling of the Forest Gene Pool. Pacific Search*, June 1976, pp. 7-9.

Stewart, Ronald E.
1977. *Statement of Ronald E. Stewart, Project Leader, Reforestation Systems in the Pacific Northwest*, USDA Forest Service, before the U.S. House of Reps. House Subcomm. on Forests, July 8, 1977, Roseburg, OR.

Terrant, Robert F. and Trappe, James M.
1971. *The Role of Alnus in Improving the Forest Environment. Plant and Soil*, special vol. 1971, MS. SVW-28.

USDA
1969. *Soil Resource Atlas, Olympic National Forest. USDA Forest Service Draft EIS [Rev.]: Vegetation Mag't.*
1977. *Pacific NW Region*, USFS, Portland, OR.

USDA-SC
1974. *Southwestern Wash. River Basins Type IV Survey, Preliminary Field Draft*, Economic Research Serv., Forest Serv. & State of Washington.

Vannote, Robin L.
1977. *The River Continuum: A Theoretical Construct for Analysis of River Ecosystems*. Contribution No. 1 from the National Science Foundation River Continuum Project.

Wolf, Robert E.
1975. *The Douglas Fir Region Timber Supply Situation and Log Export Regulation as Proposed by H.R. 5544*. Library of Congress, Congressional Research Service, Washington, D.C.

PROLOGUE: BELL FOUNDING, GROUNDING THE INTRICACIES OF AN IMAGE

In medieval times in Europe, bell founders were itinerant craftsmen who traveled from town to village stopping to ask local parishes if they needed any new bells. (In those days, bells were the sound of living. They called us to prayer, sounded alarm in fire, war and flood, pealed for joy at weddings and births or passed the dead to rest.) If work was available, the bell founder set about to gather his material, digging clay to make the bell shape (cope) and core; he requisitioned horse hair, eggs and manure to mix in with the clay to reinforce and "open" it to create a material matrix that would not break yet "breathe" when the 2,000 Fahrenheit-degree metal flowed into it. He secured the bell metal (90 percent copper and 10 percent tin) and perhaps a secret amount of gold or silver—a wedding ring to sweeten the sound. Village women piled their worn out copper and tin ware as a tithe towards the bell's realization, remembering later their broken pot became a sacred sound. The casting pit was dug, where the bell maker made the pattern. It was where the bell mold was baked dry, buried and rammed tight to hold it so it would not break apart during the metal pour. Villagers cut wood to make charcoal to bake the mold firm and melt the metal. They made brick to build the chimney melt furnace. Bells were traditionally cherished in the villages of Europe, and in times of crisis or war they were buried to keep them safe from looters or warring factions.

When the mold was baked dry and secured in the pit and the furnace charged with charcoal and metal, the bell founder and his apprentice would strike the melt and work the bellows and draft until the furnace was full of liquid metal. The founder would then tap the furnace—that is, pull the plug that allowed hundreds of pounds of metal to pour into the mold. When the bell was set and cool enough to handle, the founder would trim the bell to tune and hang it in the belfry, where it would begin its life as the voice of the town.

The clapper of a bell is traditionally called a tongue. When the tongue meets the edge of the bell, the bell speaks or sings. Every creature for miles around the village paused in the clear temple of its song, but few knew or cared about the necessities of its beauty. Traditionally, a well-cast bell allowed a blossoming stillness in the wake of its ring, one note nourished by the informed silence of a thousand storied deaths, a conspiracy of wood, ore, hair, broken pots, cracked cannon, ancient clay, new sweat, sinewed practice, bird ova and timeless incandescent fire—a celebration of life's glance into the water-polished gaze of time.

~

"The necessity of beauty" is a seemingly simple expression. It says beauty is necessary; but how? Is beauty born of necessity, hence an embedded, elemental condition of reality? Or is beauty a profound human need to experience, belonging to a world that appears as barely cadenced chaos? Perhaps it is both—our ancient alertness and creation's potent uncertainties, thin ice and fertile soil, the dreamy weave of our awareness and the world.

"The necessity of beauty." *Necessity* derives from the Latin phrase *necess est*: "it is an unavoidable task or duty—an unyielding presence, unceasing, inevitable" (Eric Partridge, *Origins: A Short Etymological Dictionary of Modern English*, MacMillan, 1977). In the shadow of necessity's etymology we might rephrase the calling of this essay "The Unceasing, Inevitable Presence of Beauty" (i.e., the world is always beauty-full) or, more subjectively, "Our Unrelenting Duty to Beauty." From necessity's deeper root perspective, beauty is an essential obligation. Beauty now appears not as the world's secret nor the soul's longing but a fateful, ever-present promise between our haunted psyches and the mysterious world around us, an atmosphere, a charge that precipitates illusion-piercing surprise. "The necessity of beauty"—the world is beauty-full, it is our duty to attend it.

The root sense of the necessity of beauty qualifies and re-imagines the ethical compass of attending beauty. The etymology of *beauty* helps us to understand the occasion of its experience: the event, the reception, the blossom, the birth, the surprise and the demise of beauty. *Beauty* derives from a diminutive form of the Latin word for good—*bonus*, hence, the diminutive *bellus*, *bella*, handsome, beautiful. *Bonus* and the Scot's *bonny* sprout from the Indo-European root *dwenos*: health, energy, strength. The Greek word *dunamis*, power, comes from this root and enters our language as *dynamic*, *dynamo*, etc. Beauty is dynamic, alive, energized, healthy, powerful. Beauty is the fateful eros of ethics and aesthetics, the electricity of mystery come to ground.

The original perception that informed our imagination of beauty has been abandoned by modern aesthetics and its arbitrary cycle of art for art's sake revolutions, where beauty suffocates in costume rather than being refreshed by custom. Postmodern aesthetics is expressed in one tired thought, "Beauty is in the eye of the beholder." This threadbare relativism has denigrated shared cultural experience. It's as if the muse were chained to your living room couch. We don't know how to attend beauty, the necessary obligation to its dynamic. We purchase beauty in products, on trips and tours. But beauty is not a luxury item, is not pretty, cute or stylish; it is alive. Of course, beauty resounds in objects and events. Their peculiar limits enliven beauty's surprise but do not explain beauty's mercurial nature. Beauty is not proprietary; it is propitious and profound.

Because our culture encourages an economically corrupt and socially atomized sense of beauty that is a clandestine vendetta of cleverness against the sacredness of creation—because we are strangers to each other and the places we live—beauty slips through the blurry witness of our shared addictions. We have lost the subliminal and sublime compass of the "necessity of beauty," so beauty dodges us like a wounded sparrow in an alley full of trash.

We no longer practice a tradition of "walking in beauty," as the old ones say. We have the habit of convenience. We flip a light switch and so neglect celebration of the sun's arrival and departure. We don't share beauty as humans have for thousands of years, rehearsing and retelling the uncanny resonances between our souls and the world, dynamically, in song and dance, in stone and wood, addressing the mutual mystery of soul and cosmos in dignity. Instead, we trick it out in a neurosis of styles.

How do you imagine beauty's informing shadow, its gravity, its necessity, its *dwenos*? I see blue sky and cloud-shadowed wind over the swaying evergreens around our home. I see ants re-thatching their colony with fir needles in spring. I recall my wife listening with gentle attention to a group of our son's friends speculating in the kitchen. Dynamic is directed vitality, a rampant stream near flood, a writhing snake in the grip of your fist. It is said that sexual ecstasy is the "little death"; maybe beauty's clear resonance, its witness, is the "little life" embracing the witness-quickened vividness of creation's mystery, "the necessity of beauty," the inner and outer dissolved in a moment, a touch, a word, a sound, a silence.

Beauty's dynamic is not perfect or ideal. It is subject to the same logos of death, decay and transformation as all creation. Who would Persephone, a lovely girl-goddess of spring, be without her husband, Hades? A silly maiden with flowers in her hair? Her real beauty, the necessity of the occasion of her beauty, requires her to spend fall and winter in the underworld loving her husband and weaving the threads of destiny. Necessary beauty has character, gravitas, sorrow, comedy and joy. Beauty without gravity may be a decorous ruse. Beauty without shadow is probably an illusion, and beauty without vitality a trap. Beauty may be stark but never vain, and joy may emerge as sorrow's final cry.

Lastly, "the necessity of beauty" invites us to consider its practice (Greek, *praktikos*, able in, fit for, active, from *prassein*, to do habitually, which is related to *pera*, over, beyond, leading over or through). Practice gets us where we need to go.

Beauty is dynamic; it's like a river or herd of horses or forest fire. We only get a glance of it coursing, swimming in and out of our awareness, running through the world. Beauty can't be controlled, invented or explained. (How long do you think the muse would stay chained to a couch?) But it may be met. Necessity is, at heart, about duty, and duty is grounded in humility. So the practice of "the necessity of beauty" is humble attendance. No grabbing, profiteering or circus side-shows allowed. If we're going to walk in beauty, our practice dwells in how we attend the world and its fellowship, ourselves included. This is humility, not humiliation. (My neighbor reported seeing a banana slug glide across his porch stop and rise up, stretching into the commencement of a light rain, waving slowly back and forth, attending the nuances of its arrival.) The practice of "the necessity of beauty" teaches us that beauty is not a personal fantasy or something "magic" in the root-slow moil of the rock-hard world. In my ragged experience, beauty is like a spark, a shock or, more truly, a resonance that blooms between our soul's ancient imagination and the world's subtle elemental working, its energies. Beauty, in my witness, is a moment when we hear the song creation sings and remember we know the tune by heart.

But let us not be deceived or conned by our love of and the comfort taken in the light, clear and vital poetics of creation, its grandeur and majesty. Perhaps we know that tune too well. There is also beauty in the terrifying storm and in the killer whale tossing the dead seal like a circus toy. There is beauty in the one-legged, insane beggar, his empty pantleg a knotted and swinging pendant beside his agile crutch while he howls defiantly, hobbling by in the shadows behind the Greyhound station.

Remember lovely Persephone and Hades; together they constellate a somber, truthful beauty; apart, they become caricatures, cartoons of mortality and joy. Beauty's fluid thread is a Mobius strip with life on one side and death on the other. Beauty's "twist" erases their division and sows us into the vivid, sometimes terrifying, fertile beauty that bears us on; we're alive, but we're going to die. Life and death sift the necessity, the beauty, out of sentiment and into soil that grows the bread we need. This is life's practice, all beings walking in beauty, the salmon dying to feed the trees. The fellowship of living beings shares a similar practice, imperfect, evolving, stutter-stepping, faithful to the screwy, spiraling, gifted story that drills through time, tracking the necessities of beauty, the beauty of necessity; death's fey wife dancing in the fields and forests, coaxing bee to blossom, calling us home.

"The necessity of beauty" is not morbid; it's grounded. Death is a fundamental necessity, and the bud of inevitable death, our mortal awareness, tempers and weights our awareness so it rings the world around us like a bell, sounds its beauty. Imagine a dead snag's pale spire, a still, vulnerable witness to the breezy, verdant dance of the spring-fresh trees. A similar silence informs our cadence, the measured fall, the rhythm of our attendance, the step, the beat, the simple, fateful courage of the heart's walk through time. This gravity transforms us into the bell's tongue, the perishing moment that sounds the necessary beauty of being.

A child knows wonder, the wide-eyed, slightly anxious, enthused curiosity of first awareness. An adult may experience wonder in the same way, but a child cannot know beauty, because a child cannot imagine mortality. Mortally tempered attention (that still snag in the green breeze) humbles our touch, transforms selfish reflection into moving connection. We can't invent or conjure beauty. It can't be tricked or captured, but we can invite it, make room for beauty's occasion. Beauty's agency is an invisible conspiracy of inner and outer circumstance that inspires us to meet the world in a resounding way, a resonance of revelation that surprises us into the fellowship of creation where we belong, bell-ringing messengers sounding beauty's necessity in a rolling peal of miracles.

The Salmon of the Heart

Speckled Dream

I went to the sea
for myself.
She fed me
health, new legs.
Perhaps a speckled dream
to wrestle in the night.

Years ago, working as a boat puller on a troller in Southeast Alaska, something happened that is an image for the beginning and end of this essay. We were fishing the Fairweather grounds off Lituya. The skipper called me to bring the landing net to his side of the boat. He was working a big king on the kill line[1] and gave me instruction on how to approach the salmon with the net. It was the biggest king I had ever seen, perhaps a hundred-pounder and too big to gaff. As I brought the net behind and under him he began to swim away—not fast but steady like a draft animal pulling a heavy load. The moment had the inexorable quality of awakening: the salmon and I were in the same world as the kill line went taut and the hundred-pound test leader snapped and the fish flashed out of sight. I recall this story to remind me that salmon is free and that these musings are only lines and hooks that hold him momentarily.

As I turn 40 and enter the second half of life, it occurs to me how like the salmon is the life of the soul. Salmon is born in a rivulet, a creek, the headwaters of some greater river. He runs to the sea for a mysterious sojourn, his flesh reddens; mature, he awakens once again to his birthplace and returns

1 A rubber line to which the leader was attached while playing the fish.

there to spawn and die. Loving and dying in the home ground resounds in us. We all want a meaningful death in a familiar locale. Salmon embodies this for us, our own loving deaths—at home in the world. Salmon dwells in two places at once—in our hearts and in the world. He is essentially the same being, the sacred salmon, salmon of the heart.

The Leaper

The doctor was explaining how sperm moved, like salmon, and how the uterus gave them hold, created "current" so they knew which way to swim. I thought, "Jesus, salmon!" and knew I was one once. It was as real as this: I could remember the slow torture of rotting still alive in a graveled mountain stream. Humped up, masked in red and green, dressed for dancing, I was Death's own delight, her hands caressing me . . . and this is the part I can't remember: whether she laughed or wept as we rolled in love.

"*Introduction*" is a word that at root means being led into the circle. Here is one last introduction to salmon. Not long ago a friend and I were sitting by Admiralty Inlet, talking. I mentioned an idea to create a sculpted "rainbow" of salmon of all species. One end of the rainbow would rise out of Puget Sound, and it would end in a well in an alder grove on the shore. My friend responded to the idea by saying, "The salmon is the soul in the body of the world." Indeed the salmon is at least the soul of this biome, this green house. He is the tutelary spirit that swims in and around us, secret silver mystery, salmon of the heart, tree-born soul[2] of our world.

---

2 Trees provide detritus, organic energy forms, to feed caddis fly and other aquatic larvae that in turn feed salmon fry. In salmon spawning areas, the upper reaches of rivers, the major energy source is forest detritus. Trees also shade the home creeks, maintaining cool water temperatures vital to salmon. The forest is mother to the salmon.

This essay depends in part on the notion that, salmon-like, language bridges subject and object worlds, inner and outer. Language is the path, the game trail, the river, the reverie between them. It shimmers there, revealing and nourishing their interdependence. Each word bears and locates our meetings with the world. A word is a clipped breath, a bit of spirit (*inspire, expire*) wherein we hear the weather. Our "tongues" taste the world we eat. At root, language is sacramental. The study of etymology reveals that language is trying to contain, remember and express the religious event at the core of our mundane awareness.[3]

The heart of language is not merely communication but consecration, each word the skin of a myth. A telling example of this is our word *resource*.

In current usage, *resource* means raw material or potential energy. We have resource planning, resource development and resource allocation. In our day *resource* denotes an energized plastic something we practice our clumsy cleverness on. But beneath current usage lies a deeper, religious information. Etymology reveals that resource derives from *surge* and *re*. *Re* means back, as in return, refund. *Surge* is a Latin-rooted word whose cognates include regal, resurrection, right and rule, among others. *Surge* is a contraction of Latin *subregere*, to rule or direct from below. In its root sense, its heart sense, resource is a recurring, directed energy sent by powers hidden from view. A *resource* surges back, sent by a hidden power. What the word knows in its heart is that *resources are sacred powers*, deities. A *resource* is the unseen river. The roots of the word tell us that they are attendable, venerable. Resources require our prayer and poise, not our machinations—the spear light

3 My bet is that very few modern "new" words will last, precisely because our age has lost the religious instinct. It is not "language" but human intelligence that has created most "new" words.

above the numinous salmon, not estuarine fish factories where managed hatchery cannibal clones, hungry ghosts of our cleverness, homeless seagoing spam, return for "processing." Part of this essay's intent is to re-awaken the religious sense nascent in language; to coax words and their objects back into the sacred realm where the resource is what we listen to and for; where our "tongues" are tasting sacramental food, and our speech is "soul food."

Mircea Eliade said in his work *The Sacred and the Profane*, "To settle territory is in the last analysis equivalent to consecrating it." We are nowhere near consecrating this place. We have destroyed the original human vision of this place, and now we are busy pillaging the *resources* that inspired it. Our culture here is prophylactic and profane, a kind of battle armor rather than careful turning and returning of the soil that the etymology of *culture* reveals. We see the world through the glass of a speeding machine whose servants we are. The locale, the *resource*, is just another road kill to quarrel over. This essay cannot stop the machine or consecrate the landscape; no one person can do that. But we can roll down a window, the *windeye*, and look into the local vision, let it see us, re-awaken our longing for connection, witness the vanity of our speed. I want to praise the sacred salmon, the salmon of the heart, shuttle of Gaia's loom, swift silver thread . . .

I once swam down the Duckabush River in a wetsuit and mask. It was during the dog salmon run, and there were a lot of fish in the river. The current ran both ways that day. I came to a deep pool where a river eddy had piled a perfect pyramid of golden alder leaves. Farther on, resting in the shallows by a large submerged snag, I was musing on what I'd seen, when I noticed a shape move behind the snag. It was a large dog salmon, splotchy gray and yellow, vaguely striped, probably a male, spawned out but alive in his eyes. We were a foot apart. I looked into his eye. He saw me but did not move. I was just another river shadow, an aspect of his dying, an aspect of his marriage, another guest at the feast. He was the eye of the *resource*, the subterranean sometime king, fish-eyed inscrutable god, alder-born elder, tutor.

The salmon of the heart is not *cuisine*; it is soul food. We are subsistence fishing in the craft of language. Everyone knows when they have a bite. Imagine what follows as hooks or cut herring, "hoochies" or knots in a net, eddies in the home stream; imagine the salmon in your heart, spawning, dying.

An Etymological Glossary of Salmon Terms:[4]

Salmon: from Latin *salmo*, from Gaullic *salmo*, "the leaping fish." Ultimately derived from Indo-European *sal* to leap; hence the cognates (words born of the same root): resiliant, exultant, exile, sally, and somersault.

Alevin: from Old French *alever*, to rear, from Latin *ad-levare*, to raise; literally: a reared one.

River: from Latin *ripa*, a river bank. Cognates are arrive, derive, rivalry. Deep in the root of this word is the Indo-European *ri*, flow, which is akin to Greek *rhein* (flow) whence Rhea, the mother of the gods. (Much of salmon's power derives from its connection to rivers, to the flow, mother of gods—silver shuttle in *Gaia's loom*.)

Anadromous: from Greek *ana*, up, and *dromos*, running. Salmon is the one who runs up. The Indo-European root is *der*, whence thread, treadle, trade, tramp, trap.

---

4 A term is in its roots a terminus, a boundary, a moment looking at the other side; a glossary is a collection of glosses, terms hard to ken; etymology is the story of the truth in words.

Redd: to put in order, to ready or arrange. Partridge, in *Origins*, has *redd* as salmon spawn from red, the color, in addition to redd, dialect English to tidy, arrange, as above. The two senses seem mixed in the salmon redd, the bed of gravel heaped over the fertile eggs. It's interesting to note that redd may be related to ride and road. (Redds like grave mounds, tumuli beneath the torrent, resurrection of the resource, cradle and the grave.)

Poach: from Middle French *pocher*, to thrust, hence to encroach upon, trespass. Probably akin to Middle Dutch *pocken*, to boast, talk, big talk, bluff. A cognate of poach is poker, the bluffing game. (A poacher pokes the resource; dangerous game.)

Spawn: from Old French *espandre*, to shed, from Latin *expandere*, to stretch, to spread out. Spawn is probably akin to *patere*, to lie open; cognates: petal and patent.

Milt: salmon sperm; Indo-European root *mel*, soft; with various derivatives referring to soft or softened materials, hence melt, mulch, bland, schmaltz and smelt (metals). (Alchemical salmon, gold in the sea, mulching the soil, melting in the rivers . . .)

Roe: salmon ovum; "hard roe" are eggs, "soft roe" is sperm, milt.

Religion: from Latin *re*, back, and *ligare*, to bind. Religion binds us back. Religion is the tie that binds. Cognates include rely, ally, obligation, ligament, lien. Our connection to salmon is religious. He binds us to a sacred world, sews us into a sacred web.

Net: from Indo-European root *nedh*, to bind or knot. Cognates include node, nexus, denouement and connection.

Troll: from Old French *troller*, to walk about, to wander. Probably akin to German *stroloh*, vagabond, and our *stroll*. The French had *trollerie*, aimless wandering of dogs. (Little boats bobbing on the great sea, hoboes.)

Fry: originates in the Indo-European word root *bhrei*, to cut, break, crumble. Hence friction, debris, fray and fry. Fry are the raveling ends of a mysterious rope.

Weir: from Old Frisian and Old Saxon, *wearian*, to defend, protect, hence to hinder others. The root sense is to warn. Cognates are guarantee, warrant, garret and warn. (Indian weirs always had a hole to let salmon through. The weir warned both ways; the *resource's guarantee*.)

Parr: a young salmon. When runs decline, the parrs sometimes spawn early. Though the origin is unknown, I propose Latin *parere*, to produce a child. Indo-European root is per, to procure, produce, prepare. (*Oxford English Dictionary* suggests a Scottish origin.)

Smolt: a young salmon entering the sea. Akin to smelt. Ultimately akin to Indo-European *mel*, soft.

Well: from Indo-European *wel*, to turn, roll, with derivatives referring to curved, enclosing objects. (The well rolls . . . the well wells.)

Tutelary: ultimate origin unknown but derived from Latin *tueri*, to guard, to watch. Cognates are tutor, tuition, intuition. Salmon is a tutelary spirit of this place. He teaches and guards our health.

"Scientists guess that Atlantic salmon migrated across the Arctic Ocean during a warm period between ice ages, and then became isolated when renewed glaciation blocked the water passage above the American or Asian land masses. Through specialization, these colonizing salmonids separated into six species, taking advantage of somewhat different niches in the North Pacific environment. The Pacific salmon developed one characteristic that separates them from the Atlantic parent stock and adds greatly to their mystique—all six species return to the river only once, dying shortly after they spawn. All salmonids prefer cold, oxygen-rich waters. They range between about forty and seventy degrees north latitude. There is considerable overlap in the individual species' ranges. Only the chum and pink salmon inhabit the rivers of Siberia and northern Alaska that empty into the Arctic Ocean, and only the chinook travel as far south as Monterey Bay, but in the middle of their range all species are represented. The exception is the cherry or masu salmon, which is found only on the Asian side of the Pacific, primarily in Japan."[5]

Nine years ago I read an essay by Freeman House entitled "Totem Salmon." It changed my life then and is the inspiration for much of this essay. His description of salmon's life cycle and behavior establishes a factual background to salmon's appeal to our imaginations. I reprint a portion of it, subtitled "Salmon Mind," as a kind of "photo"-documentary of the resource-god's dance.

Salmon Mind

There are seven varieties of salmon which range and feed in the North Pacific. At the northern extreme of their range they frequent and feed in the Bering Sea, but at the southern extreme are rarely found south of forty-one degrees. These are their names:

5 Philip Johnson, "Salmon Ranching" in *Oceans*, January-February 1982, p. 42.

Onchorynchus chavica: called *King, Chinook, Tyee, Spring, Quinnat*
Northern Hokkaido to the Sacramento River
O. kisutch: called *Coho, Silver*
Monterey Bay to the Kamchatka Peninsula
O. nerka: called *Sockeye, Red, Blueback, Nerka*
Fraser River to the Kurile Islands
O. gorbucha: called *Pink, Humpbacked, Humpie*
Klamath River to Korea
O. keta: called *Chum, Dog, Keta*
Puget Sound to Korea
O. masu: called *Cherry, Masu*
Amur River to the Pusan River of Korea
Salmo gairdneri: called *Steelhead trout*
Klamath River to the Stikine in Alaska

Salmon eggs are deposited in more or less evenly graded gravel with enough cold water running over them to maintain an even temperature but not enough to disturb the eggs. The eggs are a brilliant translucent orange-red, about the size of buckshot. Sockeyes will spawn in lakes rather than streams. A single female will deposit up to a thousand eggs in a single "redd" or nest.

After a gestation period of 50 days to three months, the "alevins" hatch out with yolk sacs still attached. The babies nestle in the gravel for several weeks until the yolk sac is gone and they have gained an inch in size. At this point, they emerge from the gravel as "fry," quick and light-shy. It is at this stage of development that life is most perilous, the small fish being vulnerable to hungry larger salmon, other fish, water birds and snakes.

The fry feed at dawn and dusk and into the night on planktonic crustacea and nymphs, growing fastest in the summer when insects are most available. Most salmon remain in lakes and streams for two years, though pinks and dogs begin their journey to the sea in the first year, as fry.

The migration to salt water is an epic event involving millions of smolt (as the little salmon are called at this stage). On the Yukon River, the journey can be as long as 1,800 miles, on the Amur 700-800. The fish travel in schools, at night, to avoid predators, following the guidance of a single, larger smolt who seems to make decisions for schools at obstructions, rapids, etc. Out of two million eggs, perhaps 20,000 fish have survived to make the migration.

On the way downstream, the smolt can be killed by 1) natural predators; 2) irrigation ditches that confuse and trip the fish; 3) undissolved human sewage; 4) turbine intakes at dams, which act as meat grinders; 5) nitrogen-rich water on the downstream side of darns; 6) wastes from pulp mills; 7) wastes from chemical plants; and 8) warm or oxygen-depleted water created by industrial flow-through.

Now the smolt will spend three to five months in estuaries and bays, gradually acclimating to salt water. They begin by feeding on zooplankton. As they grow larger and develop stronger teeth they will eat crustaceans such as shrimp (which some biologists believe colors their flesh), euphasids, amphipods, copepods, pteropods and squid.

It is at this point in the consideration of salmon that biologists begin to slide off into weary, human-centered metaphors for the talents and strengths of the fish. We are talking about the great ocean migrations of the salmon, wherein they range and feed for thousands of miles in the North Pacific, grow to maturity and navigate unerringly back to the stream of their birth on a time schedule that can be predicted to within a few days.

In general, North American salmon make this circular journey in a counterclockwise direction while Asian salmon move clockwise. Often the great schools' paths will mingle, sharing the search for food that has brought them halfway across the Pacific. Pinks make the circuit once and race home to spawn; sockeyes once each year for three or four years. The enormous schools travel at a general rate of ten miles per day until the spawning urge takes them and they increase their speed to thirty miles per day. The fish are nearly always found in the top ten meters of water during the migrations.

No one really understands the mechanisms that guide the fish through the trackless ocean and back to a specific spot at a specific time. Evidence would seem to indicate that the circuits are printed on the genes of the individual fish. It is probable that neither a consciousness common to a school nor memorized information guides them. There is, however, plenty of room for speculation. The evidence is in as of 1968:

- The migration is in a circular motion, rather than to and fro, eliminating the possibility of the fish backtracking on themselves.

- Salmon find their ways to the spawning grounds as individuals, not in schools.

- Arrival of the fish at the spawning grounds is less variable than the seasonal changes in the weather, making the use of temperature gradients as guidance cues unlikely.

- The nearly constant overcast in the far North Pacific makes celestial navigation unlikely (but not impossible).

- Migration routes tend to be across open water, even in areas where it would be easy to follow the coast, so that the use of physical landmarks is eliminated.

- The fish swim actively downstream in and across the currents of the Pacific. The currents have subtle differences in salinity, but in order to use these differences as cues, the salmon would have to group up near the edges of the streams, which they do not do.

- Seawater is an electrical conductor moving through the planet's magnetic field, thus the ocean currents generate small amounts of electrical potential. Some fish are able to detect such small amounts of voltage and there is reasonable speculation on the part of Dr. William Royce et al. that salmon may have similar receptors and use the electricity as a navigational cue.

Salmon always find their way back to the stream or lake where they were born and spawn there again, generation after generation. As they approach fresh water, they have reached the peak of their physical and instinctual genius. Fat and shining and leaping, schools will swarm restlessly at the mouths of rivers and streams, waiting for optimal conditions of run-off. They feed voraciously now, generally on herring, for they will not feed again once they enter fresh water. This is the time to take salmon for meat. The flavor and texture of the flesh is at its very best and, eaten fresh, the strength of the fish will stay with the eater.

It is likely that the salmon use their keen sense of smell to identify their home estuary and to choose the right forks as they push upstream. Biologists have run experiments on the fish at this stage of their journey, plugging the salmons' nostrils. Without a sense of smell the spawning run tends to move in a random manner and the fish get lost.

The trip upstream is an enormous effort. Even in the absence of human improvements on the rivers, cataracts, rapids and waterfalls must be overcome. In spite of obstacles, the fish travel between 39 and 90 miles a day until they have reached the spawning ground. The salmon now undergo striking physiological changes. Humpbacks will grow the hump for which they are named. Dogs grow long, sharp teeth and the upper mandible grows out and extends down over the lower. The body of the sockeye will turn fresh-blood red, its head an olive green. In general, the fish turn dark and bruised; the organism begins to consume itself, Drawing its last strength from ocean-gained fat, the flesh turns soft.

Now the salmon perform the breathtaking dance for which their entire lives have been in preparation. As they reach their spawning home, the fish pair off, male and female. A sort of courtship ensues, the male swimming back and forth over the female as she prepares the nest, rubbing and nudging her, then darting out to drive off other males. The female builds the nest with her tail, scooping out silt and smaller stones to a depth of several inches and in an area twice the length of the fish. Finally all that is left in the nest are larger stones. The crevasses and fissures between the stones will provide shelter for the eggs. The nest completed, the female assumes a rigid position over the center of it and the male approaches, curving his body up against hers. The eggs and clouds of milt are deposited simultaneously. The sperm, which stays alive in the water for seconds only, must enter the egg through a single, tiny pore or micropyle, which itself closes over in a matter of minutes. In situations where the current is extremely fast, two males will sometimes serve a single female to ensure fertilization. The nest is covered and the process is repeated for a day or a week, until the eggs are all deposited. (Males fight each other for dominance, females fight each other for territory.)

A single female will deposit from 2,000 to 5,000 eggs, but only a small percentage of these are destined to hatch. The rest are eaten by fish or birds, attacked by fungi or washed downstream.

Now the fish, already decomposing, begin to die, and within days all have finished their migration. Their bodies are thrown up on the banks of streams and rivers providing feast for bear and eagle.[6]

The Atlantic salmon, a fish like our steelhead, which does not die after spawning but returns to the sea and may spawn again, was once much more extensive, with huge runs on all the major rivers of northern Europe. Runs extended as far south as Portugal and as far north as subarctic Norway and Iceland. The fish were once so plentiful that nobility would not eat them because they were a staple of their serfs' diet. Today only Iceland, Scotland, Norway and Ireland have decent salmon fisheries. England is trying to coax salmon back into its polluted waterways with varied success. The fish is essentially extinct in the rest of Europe except for a small one-river run in Normandy that is being poached into extinction despite official efforts to save it.

Compared to its European cousin, the wild Pacific salmon is in relatively good shape. But it is by no means a healthy resource. Logging has blocked streams, even whole rivers for a while. Soil failures, siltation and slope failures caused by clearcutting have destroyed spawning habitat. Overfishing has depleted breeding stocks, and dams have exterminated whole races of salmon. The most recent threat to the wild Pacific salmon is genetic contamination and competition from aquaculture clones that threaten to contaminate and/or starve out a gene pool adapted to the essential climatic and geologic variables of this locale. Clone salmon are genetically adapted to the economic and technically determined environs of state and corporate aquaculture centers. Hatchery fish are virtually different beings from wild fish. They are selected

6 "Totem Salmon" by Linn House, *Truck 18, Biogeography Workbook (1)*, Truck Press, Seattle, 1978.

for their ability to survive the crowded, *single feed* hatchery environment. (Wild salmon survive life in the ocean at twice the rate of hatchery clones since they are better adapted to natural conditions.) Aquaculturists brag of the differences. They are breeding salmon to work for corporate interests, efficient production and high profit . . . in short, breeding salmon as anadromous Herefords. Soon there may be salmon with corporate names: *Ore-Aqua silvers, Anadromous kings, Weyerhauser dogs* (all names of aquaculture corporations).

Corporate fish biologists often use the buffalo-cattle analogy when discussing wild and hatchery salmon.[7] The plains were cleared of wild herbivores so the cattle industry could grow. Corporations interested in aquaculture argue that we needn't worry about habitat or spawning grounds, that they can do it all at the river mouths with technology and money. That means that watershed health is no longer essential to salmon livelihood and that watersheds may be indiscriminately developed. This may be part of the reason why timber companies are investing in salmon aquaculture. Perhaps they figure if they can keep salmon on the industrial consumer's dinner plate, the "consumers" won't yell so loudly when logging devastates wild salmon habitat.

An interesting aspect of the wild vs. hatchery salmon issue is the carrying capacity controversy. Some biologists have begun to argue that there is a limited carrying capacity for salmon in the ocean (common sense vs. the profiteer apologists again). They predict that heavy releases of clone salmon may further reduce the food of wild salmon. (Russia and Japan have extensive hatchery programs.) What the aquaculturists are creating is an "economy" that is exploitive, and hence unstable, in place of one that was/is highly productive,

7 Much of what follows is from Philip Johnson's excellent article, "Salmon Ranching," in the January/ February 1982 issue of *Oceans*.

self-regulated and self-maintained. Wild salmon are a much more productive resource than phony resources like corporate aquaculture. Their drawback, from the corporate viewpoint, is that they cannot be manipulated and hence serve a market economy. Wild salmon have too many connections, too many harmonies. They are the thread of a story that is destroyed, taken out of context. Hatchery fish are comic book versions of epics . . . the Muzak version of a complex traditional tune. Of course, corporate and state aquaculturists pay lip service to wild salmon stocks as gene pool reserves.

But the whole thrust of modern aquaculture is to "co-operate" with the industrial, not the ecological, economy. Consciously or unconsciously they are working to eliminate the wild salmon, the salmon of the heart. Fishermen of various disciplines—trollers, gillnetters, sportsmen—know the difference between wild and domesticated salmon. Their word for hatchery fish is "rag." (Washington State is beginning to pay attention to the importance of maintaining wild runs through habitat restoration and protection.)

The decline of the wild Pacific salmon, especially the far-swimming chinook and the estuary-loving dogs, is tragic because it means the whole ecosystem is in decline. The salmon is the crown of the northwest forest biome, the soul of our ecosystem. It is, with cedar, the paradigmatic expression of this place. If the forests and their waters are healthy, if the sea is clear and uncrowded, then wild salmon thrive.

The salmon is a kind of current between forest and sea.[8] One study shows that salmon may accumulate rare trace minerals (boron?) that, passed on through the forest food

8 A Nisqually spokesman once made the Thurberesque remark that he saw salmon leaking out of all the lightbulbs, probably because dams have destroyed so many runs.

chain, provide chemical materials for green plants that are unavailable to them through local geologic and hydrologic processes. In other words, the trees nurture salmon and salmon nurture trees (alchemical salmon turning sea into soil, salmon eyes in the treetops). The salmon is the archetypal resource—meaningful energy directed by unseen powers. It is the incarnation of the forest-sea connection, silver needles sewing the ties that bind, religious fish . . . The salmon travels in our hearts as well, swims in our blood, feeds and eats the dreaming tree of truth. The deep resonance between the salmon of the heart and the salmon of the world is the note of our dwelling here.

Well
An old Bavarian farmer told me
if I was unlucky
and could not take my water
from a stream,
I might keep a trout in my well
and the water would stay clean.

The salmon is a powerful symbol of the interdependence of the outer world, but it is, as an image, also a manifestation of our inner health. Indeed the resolution of the two images, salmon of the forest and salmon of the heart, may be the inception of a healing myth. Jung associated fish with the nourishing influence of the unconscious (salmon comes from the sea to feed the locale). The alchemical stone, symbol of the immortal self, is said to appear like fish eyes. (The salmon knows the way home through the chaos of waters. Von Uexkell, a German ethologist, experimented with salmonids to determine their inner time and discovered they see twice as much per second as we do. Their world is hence much "slower" than ours.[9])

9 Is salmon "time" a key to their uncanny navigational abilities?

I once saw a rain cloak made of an enormous king salmon. The head was made into a kind of cap and the body draped over the shoulders. It was worn in the river drizzle while spearing salmon. I imagine it moving the wearer into salmon time, making the swift salmon walk. I imagine it decoding the rain. In Babylonian mythology there was a figure, Oannes, who came from the sea dressed as a fish to teach the people wisdom. Fish are symbols of wisdom throughout the world. What we fail to realize in our culture of alienated self-conscious rationalism is that fish, salmon in our case, are literal *embodiments* of the wisdom of the locale, the resource. The salmon are the wisdom of the northwest biome. They are the old souls, worshipful children of the land. *Psychology without ecology is lonely* and vice versa. The salmon is not merely a projection, a symbol of some inner process; it is rather the embodiment of the soul that nourishes us all.

We love salmon; it is the northwest *food*. But to the original peoples of the Pacific Northwest, salmon were not merely food. To them, salmon were people who lived in houses far away under the sea. Each year they undertook to visit the human people because the Indian peoples always treated them as honored guests. When the salmon people traveled, they donned their salmon disguises and these they left behind perhaps in the way we leave flowers or food when visiting friends. To the Indians the salmon were a resource in the deep sense, great generous beings whose gifts gave life. The salmon were energy: not "raw" energy, but intelligent, perceptive energy. The Indians understood that salmon's gift involved them in an ethical system that resounded in every corner of their locale. The aboriginal landscape was a democracy of spirits where everyone listened, careful not to offend the resource they were a working part of.

The salmon was to the Indians what oil is to us. And while oil is a non-renewable resource, a "non-renourishable resource," and hence perhaps not a true *resource* at all, the salmon was a true resource and was paid great heed by aboriginal peoples. In Fraser River Salish mythology, the wife of Swanset, the creator spirit, was a sockeye salmon. In western terms we might say, "The organizing principle of the world was married to the salmon." Human life was bound to the salmon. Swanset lived at his wife's village and ate with them. In the evening, when Swanset's wife and her brothers and sisters went to the river to bathe, his wife's mother could come up from the riverside, carrying a fish in her arms as if it were a child. She cooked it and, laying it on a layer of Indian consumption[10] plant, summoned Swanset and his wife to eat. Swanset's wife scrupulously washed her hands before she sat down and warned Swanset to do likewise. Her parents admonished him not to break the salmon bones but to lay them carefully on one side. When Swanset and his wife had eaten and washed their hands again, the mother-in-law gathered up all the bones and carried them to the riverside. When she returned from the river, a young boy followed, skipping and dancing gaily in circles around her. This happened at each meal. The salmon people loved to see the skipping boy; he was a joy to them.

Swanset was careless and lost a bone. The boy appeared that evening limping after the grandmother. This made the salmon people sad and after much effort the bone was found and returned to the water, whereupon the boy was made whole, and the people were glad again. This is the native understanding of the salmon. When the salmon bones are respected they experience life as a young boy dancing around an old woman. The wife of the human imagination (Swanset) was the salmon, their harmony symbolized in the young boy and old woman. Food tells a story—food has eyes, fish eyes. "Is this our body?"

10 So named because of its curative properties.

One ritual common to all native American peoples who ate salmon was the first salmon welcoming ceremony. As mentioned above, Indian peoples believed that "salmon is a person living a life very similar to the people who catch him. The salmon has a chief who leads them up the streams during the run. In performing the ceremony for the one actually caught first, they believe that they are also honoring the chief of the salmon."[11]

In the Indian view, salmon is endowed with a conscious spirit. It can present itself in abundance or not appear at all. This belief required special treatment for all living things and hence many taboos evolved to ensure safe relations with them. Below I list some northwest taboos and customs associated with salmon.[12]

1. The Klallam, like most tribes that use salmon extensively, have a certain veneration for the fish and mark its coming in the spring with a ceremony. The first fish is handled with great care. After being cut along the two sides, the parts are laid together again and it is hung with the head up. The first fish is boiled into a soup, and all the people of the village partake of it except the host. The cooking is done by the host's wife.

2. The Klallam of Beecher Bay share the British Columbian custom of performing this ceremony for the sockeye salmon, which is considered the most important variety. When the first sockeye is caught, the little children sprinkle their hair with down, paint their faces and put on white blankets. They go out to the canoe and carry the fish on their arms as though they were carrying an infant. A woman cuts it with a mussel-shell knife, after which the fish is boiled and given only to

11 Erna Gunther, *Further Analysis of the First Salmon Ceremony*, p. 156.

12 Erna Gunther, *Klallam Folk Tales*.

the children to eat. The sockeye is just like a person, they say; that is why they must be careful. This ceremony is an example of acculturation, for the procedure is identical with that of the Vancouver Island people and not at all like that of the other Klallam.

3. When a salmon with a crooked mouth is caught it is regarded as an omen of a dreadful occurrence. To forestall this they boil the fish and let all the children of the village eat some of it. Then the backbone is taken to the end of the village and set up on a pole facing the water. The other bones are thrown into the water. Another informant speaking of the same occurrence limited special treatment to the dog salmon only. A dog salmon with a crooked lower jaw is called *suxqwxtaiyuk*. Such a fish is boiled, the backbone removed, and then it is roasted, being spread open with cross pieces of ironwood (oceanspray). It is eaten only by young people, who save every bone very carefully. When they are through eating they all go to the water with the salmon bones, dive under the water and release the bones. The fish is treated this way because it is considered the leader of the salmon and must therefore be shown respect so that the run will not cease.

4. When a boy catches his first salmon, his grandmother, or in case she is dead, some other woman past her climacteric, cleans the salmon, boils it and eats it. Only old people are permitted to eat of it. The bones are thrown into the water.

5. Children are always admonished not to play with salmon that are lying around before being cleaned. If they tamper with the eyes or make fun of the fish they will get sick and act like the salmon when it is dying. A girl of about ten was swimming in the Dungeness River and made fun of an old salmon. Soon after, she became ill. Her eyes began to look like salmon eyes and her actions were just like the movements of the fish as they swim. Her people asked her if she had played

with a salmon. She admitted that she had. The shaman could do nothing for her and she soon died.

6. It is the common belief that the old salmon come back to lead the young ones up the river. Some young men who had just been initiated into the secret society doubted this. They found a very old salmon, almost dead, on the bank of the river. The boys took off some of their ceremonial headdress and tied it to the fins and tail of the fish. Then they pushed him into the river, saying, "If you are the one who leads the young salmon back we will see you again next year." The next salmon season the young men went to the place where they had marked the salmon and found the old fish with strips of their headdress. After they had seen this they became ill. The shaman could not help them. When they were dying, they acted like dying salmon.

7. Each season new poles are made for drying salmon. It is believed the salmon play on these poles while they are drying and new poles make them happy. They are always treated as if they are alive.

8. Bones of salmon are burned or thrown into water.

9. Hearts of salmon are burned to keep them away from dogs.

10. Care is taken not to break bones.

11. Eyes are eaten.

12. People in close relation to death, puberty, birth are prevented from eating salmon.

13. Children are rubbed from throat to belly with the fat of first salmon.

14. It was believed that twins were salmon people and had power to call salmon and increase runs.

15. People of Twana Fjord (Hood Canal) prohibited garbage dumping and boat bailing during times when salmon were running.

To the original Northwest people, salmon was a *resource* in the sense that the roots of our language perceive *resource*, that which is resurgent and regal. Salmon is an aspect of the ordering power of creation and must be respected. Salmon has a fateful connection to death, birth and puberty. It is a manifestation of the power of the other side. All biological systems are dependent on death, the detritus pathways, for health. We are nourished on death, supported by it, the way the dead heart of a tree holds it up in the light. Death is the sinew of the soul. There is a Nootkan tradition wherein the chief swims up-river towing skeletons of various fish to entice them back into the river. That salmon were eternal and moved between both worlds was a worldwide belief. Maybe salmon are a manifestation of the spirit world's migration through ours; radiant beings leaving us their warmth, their cloaks, the *blossom* of their souls. It is no wonder that Northwest Indian peoples saw twins as "salmon born" and ascribed to them power to increase and predict runs. Twins are the literal expression of nature's ambivalence, the revelatory power of coincidence. Twins seem more "fated" than other children. People close to the power of the other side—children, widows, menstruating women, new fathers and mothers—had restricted relations with salmon. It was as if they were closer to and hence more vulnerable to the *resource*.

Researching this essay I discovered that the *flash* in our phrase "flash of inspiration" is etymologically grounded not in lightning but in the flash-splash of a fish. Ideas do not flash like lightning but rise like trout to caddis flies. Deep in our speech is the notion that fish are prescient witnesses to the cosmos. They are quick, as in *quickened*, *quicksand*, or that tender flesh beneath your fingernail. Each year the silver salmon return to the little creek that runs through the forest south of my home. I marvel at their speed and freshness and how they sense my presence long before I see them. My witness is always of them disappearing, flashing shadows. It is hard to imagine anyone hunting them with a spear. On the other side, the eternal salmon was a daily witness to the Indians' life. It played in the drying racks while gear was mended, berries gathered. We fail to realize how intimate the Indians, especially Indian women, were with the salmon. To dry salmon properly the women had to knead the flesh to break the fibers and allow air to enter. But the fish were "alive," *conscious* until eaten. The Indian world was so particularly animate that individual crows that Klallam women shooed away from the drying racks had names. Contrast our world-view in which resources are inanimate, soulless, "dead," because they are nonhuman, and the native (Indian, Ainu, Irish, Finn, etc.) view in which everything is alive; even the strips of meat in the alder smoke can play, know joy.[13] This is not sentimentality or naiveté on the natives' part. It is a deep recognition of a resource's true nature. The bright light of our *objectivity* (ironic word) has eliminated the shadows, the shades. Even after contact with the whites gave them unlimited access to blade steel, the Indians continued to clean and dress the first salmon with the old mussel knife out of respect. It is as if we are overly enamored with the sharpness of our knives, in love with cutting. Our science, our knowing, lacks religion, reverence. We can cut the world apart but forget to call it home, and we are left alone with arid technical skills and their attendant bad dreams.

13 Can an industrially canned salmon dance?

The native peoples of the Northwest believed that orphans and others who have fared badly socially will get the best spirit guides because they will make the greatest effort to receive them. Our pride and greed have orphaned us from the earth inside and out. The tragedy is that we don't know it. We are proud of our isolation; we call it progress. The spirits are offended by our pride and avoid us, amplifying our loneliness until it becomes our *secret reason for self-destruction*.

The salmon was sacred to many peoples of the Pacific rim. The indigenous people of Japan, the Ainu, had a belief system similar to Northwest coast people. In the Ainu world, everything is a *Kamui*, a spirit of natural phenomena. In their world the Kamui are Ainu, but when they come to this world they disguise themselves as salmon, bear, deer, etc. They bring this disguise as a gift to the Ainu. The Kamui are not ghosts but eternal spirits. Some researchers report that the Ainu believed that Ainu who lived well went to Kamui Land when they died. Because the Ainu experienced the Kamui as eternal people in the beings around them, the Ainu world is a humane place, and right human behavior—care, politeness, cleanliness—assured the Ainu that the Kamui would reside in Ainu locales and enliven their world. To the Ainu, life depends on good relations with the resource world, not on owning it. The Ainu and Northwest Indians knew that *resources* can't be owned any more than a Christian can own the Holy Ghost.

The Ainu believed that the house fire was an eye of the Kamui that watched and welcomed all game that entered through the hunting window. As game entered through the hunting window, the fire reported its treatment back to the appropriate Kamui community. Fire is the appropriate witness for the resource, flickering warm light rising from the broken limbs of trees. (The leaves of the cottonwood trees were the *food* of the salmon Kamui.[14]) The mythic images circle and knot together into a reality that is a story, a parable, where facts are legendary incidents, not data.

For the Ainu, river systems were families—major rivers, parents, and the tributaries, children. One could address the whole family by speaking to a member. You could address a whole watershed, its *being*, by invoking the main river-Kamui.

The Ainu cooked the first dog salmon and offered it to the fire spirit so it would report salmon's kind treatment. The bones were offered to the river spirit with other offerings so that all spirits involved in salmon's arrival were acknowledged. The Ainu also had a send-off ritual with which they bid the salmon spirits farewell as they journeyed in their boats back to Kamui Land. These rituals are described in more detail in Hitoshi Watanabe's *The Ainu Ecosystem*, which gives a thorough explication of their cosmology. It seems to me that modern ecologists have yet to *find* language that approaches the compact imagery of native peoples whose myths not only explain the workings of ecosystem ethics but *locate* the people in the story, *instruct* us.

River Song

I lay cold
and sleek
in that swift river.

The sun sang small
faint rainbows round
all there was to see.

---

14 Intuitive knowledge of detritus pathways?

I lay still like a fish
letting my body dream.

Waiting I lay watching
my quick dogs stalking
earnest on the shore.

I lay bright and dumb
as a stone
and while the river sang
I listened to my heart.
He sounded strong and far away.
He sounded like a man digging slowly
in a half-finished well.

As mentioned above, European peoples have a long association with salmon. In fact, if philologists are right, salmon have been with us from the beginning. Calvin Watkins, in a fascinating essay in the *American Heritage Dictionary*, "Indo-European and the Indo-Europeans," notes that we can tell much about the homeland of our linguistic ancestors from the roots of our language. In the Indo-European homeland there were, among others, wasp, bee, bear, wolf, mouse, eagle, thrush, sparrow, crane, eel and salmon. The Indo-European root word for salmon is *laks*, whence our word lox. (Our word *salmon* is from Latin *salire*, to leap.) Some interesting etymological coincidences constellate around *laks*, and while my thoughts are speculative, I offer them in hope that someone more skilled will comment on them. *Laks* is the root word for salmon. The root word for lake is *laku*. From this root word we have lagoon, lough, lacuna. It seems possible that *laks* and *laku* are related. Salmon could be "laks," the lake dweller. It is interesting that *laku* gives us Latin *lacuna*, originally a pool or cistern; Celtic myth has the salmon of wisdom living in a well. Last, there is the Old English dialectic "to lake," to play or sport, from Old Norse *leig*, to leap or tremble. It is a thin line, but salmon may be animating that word. (How sad that the animals are leaving our language as they leave our lives.) In any case the salmon was a sacred fish to our ancestors, who saw him in lakes, coming and going, a mysterious being. The sacrality survives in various ways—the aboriginal Finns found fire in the bowels of the salmon, the salmon's flesh being a form of fire. To the Norwegians, a happy person is a "glad Laks," a glad salmon. The Celtic peoples venerated the salmon as the fish of wisdom until Christian times, and numerous folktales continue to bear witness to its sacrality.

Hunter's Song
Striking,
stricken.
An eagle with a fish too big to lift.
I answer from my place.

In Celtic mythology there was a sacred well of inspiration and wisdom surrounded by hazels, whose blossoms or fruit fall into the well and are eaten by the sacred salmon, whose bellies turn purple from the color of the fruit. The salmon ate the fruit of the tree of wisdom and hence knew all. Remember that a flash of inspiration is more like the splash of a fish than a bolt out of the blue.

The Welsh hero Mabon was once captured by a fiend. Gwryhr, his wife, asked the creatures to help her find him. She asked ouzel, who sent her to owl, who sent her to eagle, who, though he flew highest and saw farthest, could not find him. The eagle told Gwryhr this story: "I once tried to capture a large salmon but he drew me into the deep and I was barely able to escape.[15] I sent my kindred to attack him but he sent messengers and we made peace. I took fifty fish spears from his back. He will know where your husband is if anyone does." Eagle took Gwryhr to salmon, who located her husband. In Celtic cosmology the salmon is the wisest of all the creatures.

The wife of Dagda, the good god in the ancient Irish cosmology, was driven by curiosity to approach the forbidden well of Boann, the well of wisdom with its hazels and salmon. All the creatures of the cosmos, even the gods, were forbidden access to this well. Only the salmon were permitted to eat of the well fruit. The Irish called them the salmon of knowledge. As Dagda's wife approached the well, it rose up in anger and rolled away to the sea, freeing the salmon and creating the River Boyne. The gods may be powerful but they are not wise. Only salmon are privileged to wisdom.

Finn, the Irish hero, happened upon an old man fishing by a deep pool in the Boyne. This old man was Finn the Seer; he had been fishing seven years for the salmon of knowledge. It was prophesied that a man named Finn would obtain its wisdom. Finn the Seer caught the salmon the moment before young Finn's arrival. He gave the salmon to Finn to cook, warning him not to eat any of the fish but to only cook it and return it to the old man, who planned to eat it all and gain its wisdom. When Finn returned with the cooked salmon the seer asked him if he had eaten any part of the fish. Finn answered, "No, but while I was cooking it a blister rose on its skin. I put my thumb on it, but it burned me and I put my thumb in my mouth to cool." "It is enough," said Finn the Seer. "Eat the fish yourself. You must be the Finn of the prophecy." Thereafter Finn had only to put his thumb

15 Most salmon fishers have seen eagles swimming in the sea, unable to lift off with their catch.

in his mouth to gain knowledge of the spot he was in at the moment. It seems that the salmon of knowledge is available to the innocent and lucky.

The Irish folk tale "Country Under the Waves" is a charming story about a peasant family's fate, the well of wisdom and its tutelary animal, the salmon. (Charm is etymologically akin to *cirm*, Old English for clamor, cry, and to Latin *carmen*, song. Originally, charm meant a magic spell that was sung.) In the story a widow has three sons and a daughter. One of the sons is a dunce and the mother despairs of his future when she can no longer care for him. She consults a witch who advises her to visit the country under the waves where the hazel-ringed well of wisdom and the salmon are located. The witch instructs her to send her eldest son to obtain the hazel fruit on All Hallowed Eve when there is an "opening" in the world and he can pass into the country under the waves.[16] The eldest son undertakes his journey at the proper time and passes into the country under the waves where he meets the sea people who offer to help him. He accepts their hospitality but offends them with his bragging ways. The sea people evidently decide he is not worthy of the fruit of wisdom so they drug his food and he falls asleep at the well and turns to stone as the berries fall and the waters and salmon rise to eat them. A similar fate befalls the second brother, who goes the next year in search of the well and its fruit. He is lazy and selfish and so he is drugged and turns to stone waiting at the well. The widow's daughter pleads with her to let her make the quest for the well fruit. Her mother refuses on the grounds that she is her only whole child and she could not bear her loss. But on the next All Hallowed Eve the daughter steals away to the country under the waves. She too meets the sea people, whom she impresses with her ready wit and good manners. They guide her to the

16 Another example of pagan cosmology: resourceful submerged, persistent beneath the Christian overlay.

well where she catches the fruit before it falls to the rising salmon. Enlightened by the touch of the well fruit, she lifts the curse from her stoned brothers and returns home with them to cure their foolish brother. Evidently the wisdom of the salmon is properly won by a feminine spirit, the subtle path of right relations, rather than by bulling through or cutting through.

Following salmon is a winding path. The image is knotted in us like a nerve. But in our pose of modernity we do not know this. We waterski on the clear dark waters of Creation. But it is time to let salmon home again to our brook hearts, well hearts. "Old quartz nose," embodiment of wisdom, silver shadow, far-ranging flash of the sea, tree ghost, silver needle sewing our world together, mending the coat we wear, shuttle of dreams . . . sacred salmon, moon-bright tutor who teaches death is the door to love. If salmon disappear the splashing and flashing in the well will frighten us and we will become superstitious about the earth and our dreams. We need salmon to remind us; we are not alone.

Last, I want to offer an Estonian folksong, *The Wonder Maiden from Fish*. Estonians are a Finno-Ugric people who have lived in the same locale for perhaps eight thousand years. They have maintained their language and traditions despite crusading Germans, imperialistic Swedes and totalitarian Russians. It was the women in Estonia who kept the folklore alive. They were the singers; songs were passed from songstress to songstress—charms smoothed and polished like sacred stones. My mother-in-law, Silva Peek, a Finno-Ugric philologist who clarified a folklore text and German translation of that song, says it is probably part of an Estonian folksong tradition wherein a fish turns into a maiden. The song and its levels deserve longer treatment; still, it speaks for itself quite well. For me it is a kind of bell tone of the salmon of the heart, a shape to hold these disparate yet connected notes. It rings true.

Silva explained that this particular song is a kind of "nonsense" song wherein the original Estonian lines are joined by alliteration and rhyme rather than by any consciously chosen meaning, its shape and form worked by the unconscious wisdom of the people. This is precisely its *charm*. I hear the salmon singing through the wonder maiden, its wisdom and desire gliding bare beneath the surface of her song,[17] resurgent, the *resource* singing through human voice.

The Wonder Maiden from Fish
The spruce stands high in Kurland,
The alder, free and affable in Westernland,
The birch in Harrien beside the cow path:
Together their roots run,
Together the tops fall.
From below the roots a river flows,
Three kinds of fish therein:
One is whitefish, the blacksided one,
The other is pike, the graybacked,
The third is salmon, the wide blazed one.
I took the fish into my hand;
Carried the fish home myself.
I began cooking the fish
With the help of Father's well-stocked woodpile,
With the help of Mother's broad shavings.
The fish began to speak, saying:
"I wasn't brought up to be brutalized
Nor brought up to be roughed up.
Why, I was brought up to sing,
To sing to rhyme.
I sing, why wouldn't I?

17 I have given Silva's translation nearly verbatim, changing only a few words for rhythmic reasons.

I sing turf out of the sea,
Tilth out of sea bottom,
Fish from sea shores,
Malt from sea sand.
I sing the meaning of some other tongue
Helper of teeth."

Bibliography

Clark, Ella Elizabeth. *Indian Legends of Canada*. Toronto: McClelland and Stewart Limited, 1960.

Elmendorf, Richard. *The Structure of Twana Culture*. Seattle: Washington State University, 1960.

Evans-Wentz, W. Y. *The Fairy Faith in Celtic Countries*. Princeton: Humanities Press, 1977.

Ford, Patrick. *The Mabinog; and Other Medieval Welsh Tales*. Los Angeles and Berkeley: University of California Press, 1977.

Gunther, Erna. *A Further Analysis of the First Salmon Ceremony*. Seattle: University of Washington Press, 1930.

_____, *Klallam Ethnography*. Seattle: University of Washington Press, 1927.

_____, *Klallam Folk Tales*. Seattle: University of Washington Press, 1925.

House, Linn. "Totem Salmon" in *Truck 18, Biogeography Workbook (1)*. St. Paul: Truck Press, 1978.

Jay, T. E. "The Leaper" and "Well" previously unpublished.

_____, "Speckled Dream," "River Song" and "Hunter's Song" from *River Dogs*. Port Townsend: Copper Canyon Press, 1976.

Johnson, Phillip. "Salmon Ranching" in *Oceans* (a publication of the Oceanic Society), 15:1 (1982).

Lockley, Ronald. *Animal Navigation*. New York: Hart Publishing Society, 1967.

Loorits, Oskar. *Basics in Estonian Folkbeliefs III*. Lund (Sweden): 1957.

McGerry, Mary. *Great Fairy Tales of Ireland*. New York: Avenel Books, 1976.

Partridge, Eric. *Origins: A Short Etymological Dictionary of Modern English*. New York: Greenwich House, 1983.

Squire, Charles. *Celtic Myth and Legend*. London: Newcastle Publishing Co., 1975.

Vannote, Robin, *The River Continuum: A Theoretical Construct for Analysis of River Systems*. Contribution #1 from N.S.F. River Continuum Project, Stroud Water Research Center, Academy of Natural Sciences of Philadelphia, Mondale: 1984.

Watanabe, Hitoshi. *The Ainu Ecosystem*. Seattle: University of Washington Press, 1972.

Woodcock, George. *Peoples of the Coast: The Indians of the Pacific Northwest*. Edmonton (Canada): Jurtig Publications, 1977.

Acknowledgements

Poems and essays in this collection first appeared thanks to: Copper Canyon Press, *Montana Gothic, AAG-AAG, Upriver/ Downriver, Environmental and Architectural Phenomenology Newsletter, Connotations, Empty Bowl Firecrackers #1, Working the Woods/Working the Sea: Dalmo'ma* 6, and Alaska NW Books

"Prologue to Ohode R.A.R.E. II Proposal" was first published in *Dalmo'ma* 2 in 1978 by Empty Bowl.

"The Necessity of Beauty" first appeared in *Connotations: The Island Institute Journal* (Spring 2007) published by The Island Institute in Sitka, Alaska. Information on the Institute and its programs may be found on the web at www.islandinstitutealaska.org. *American Arts Quarterly*, Winter 2008, volume 25, no. 1

The Bowlers

Many thanks to the friends of the ever-emptying bowl who have contributed financial support to produce this and other Empty Bowl titles, and whose generosity is responsible for the very existence of this press:

Larry Laurence

Jewell Atwell

Bill Porter

Kevin Quigley

Duke Rhodes

Clemens Starck

Paul Nelson

John Pierce & Holly Hughes

Finn Wilcox & the late and deeply missed Pat Fitzgerald

Empty Bowl is forever indebted to those friends who have always supported Empty Bowl's projects with enthusiasm, editorial finesse and astute advice:

Tim McNulty

Jack Estes

Jeremiah Gorsline

Art Goodtimes

Steven R. Johnson

Jennifer Westdal

Joseph Bednarik

Eli Barrett

Bill Yake

Bill Ransom

Finally, a bow of gratitude to Mike O'Connor for his wisdom in bringing out Tom Jay's previous collection when he breathed life back into Empty Bowl.